The Collected Works
of

EDITH STEIN

Sister Teresa Benedicta of the Cross
Discalced Carmelite
1891-1942

Volume Three

The Collected Works of

EDITH STEIN

Sister Teresa Benedicta of the Cross
Discalced Carmelite

Volume Three

ON THE PROBLEM OF EMPATHY

Third Revised Edition

Translated by Waltraut Stein, Ph.D.

ICS Publications
Washington, D.C.
1989

ICS Publications
2131 Lincoln Road, N.E.
Washington, D.C. 20002

Typeset and Produced in the United States of America

Cover photo: Edith Stein at home in Breslau, 1921.
Courtesy of Cologne Carmel.

Library of Congress Cataloging-in-Publication Data

Stein, Edith, 1891–1942.
On the Problem of Empathy.

(The collected works of Edith Stein ; v. 3)
Translation of: Zum Problem der Einfühlung.
Includes index.
1. Empathy.   2. Phenomenological psychology.
I. Title.   II. Series: Stein, Edith, 1891–1942. Works. English. 1986 ; v. 3.
B3332.S672E54   1986   vol. 3   193 s [128'.3]   89-1949
ISBN 0-935216-11-1

CONTENTS

ON THE PROBLEM OF EMPATHY

Chapter II. **The Essence of Acts of Empathy**

Contents   vii

ON THE PROBLEM OF EMPATHY

Foreword to the Third Edition

Translation is always a difficult task. It calls for a high order of intellectual virtue, demanding expertise in languages and in the art of interpretation. Dr. Waltraut Stein gives evidence in this work of these competencies and especially of the ability to penetrate and transmit empathically the text of her great-aunt's work *On the Problem of Empathy (Zum Problem der Einfühlung)*. This statement is no mere play on words but is meant rather to express the translator's human understanding and rapport with Edith Stein's thought. This is the first reason why I was happy to learn that a third edition of the translation was projected and why I readily agreed to write a brief preface. In my research and writing on E. Stein's philosophy, I have used the second edition extensively and regretted that the book was not available to many others because it was out of print.

Another reason why I welcome the new edition is the important place that this work occupies in E. Stein's philosophy and in the development of phenomenology. Anyone who wishes to penetrate her thought should begin with this early work. It sketches the broad outlines of her philosophy of the human person, details of which she fills in in subsequent investigations. For her, the awareness *that* empathy is and of *what* it is are linked essentially with the understanding of the "I" as person, and a way of understanding person is through descriptive analyses of empathy. By means of the latter, she gives what may be called a first draft of the psycho-physical-spiritual nature of person, one which is not superficial but which raises many questions to be addressed in her future works. It was E. Stein's conviction that phenomenology was the most appropriate approach to the investigation of the structure of the human person, and she gave it her best efforts throughout her scholarly career.

This work, which was her Ph.D. dissertation, reveals both in method and content the breadth, depth, and precision of her philosophizing even at the beginning of her career. It reveals also something of the enthusiasm and excitement which she, one of Edmund Husserl's most brilliant pupils, experienced in the laborious research and writing that was required. Even at this time, in preparing a dissertation which had to win the "Master's" approval, Edith displays an originality and independence of thought that anticipated later existential developments in phenomenology. Not only does she differ from Husserl—albeit diplomatically—in some respects, but she also takes issue with some theories of Scheler, T. Lipps, Münsterberg, and others of her contemporaries, in the process of formulating her own theory.

In addition to the translation of the text and the valuable footnotes, the translator has supplied an introduction which gives readers an excellent entrée into the thought world of the phenomenologists of the time. Within the space of a few pages, she gives a helpful introduction into the Husserlian viewpoint which influenced E. Stein and into the organization and significance of the various sections of the text. In the final section of her introduction, she raises a question regarding whether E. Stein holds an unjustifiable assumption concerning the type of rationality which values and feelings have. This is an example of an issue which seems to me to be elucidated later in the *Beiträge zur philosophischen Begründung der Psychologie und der Geisteswissenschaften [Contributions to the Philosophical Grounding of Psychology and the Cultural Sciences]* published in 1922. It is a question that may be legitimately raised on the basis of this first work.

Finally, it should be noted that the book has the potential to be useful to scholars in psychology. E. Stein's own studies in psychology before concentrating on phenomenology appear to have been of great value to her in this and later works, in which the analyses of human experiences are a springboard to an understanding of the nature of the human person.

Mary Catharine Baseheart, S.C.N.
M.A., Ph.D.

Spalding University
Louisville, Kentucky
September, 1988

Preface to the Third Edition

W hen the Institute of Carmelite Studies asked me to pre-
pare a new edition of my translation of Edith Stein's
doctoral dissertation for their series of her collected works in
English, I was delighted to do so, because a wider audience will
now have the opportunity to examine a young scholar's rigorous
and technical work in the light of her later reputation as a power-
ful and revered spiritual giant.

At this time, about thirty years after presenting this translation
as my thesis for the degree of Master of Philosophy, I find myself
again drawn to my great-aunt's work, this time as a guide to living
the Christian life fully and deeply. I am struck by the fact that she
returned to scholarly work in a new way after her conversion to
Christianity and continued in this work for the remainder of her
life. This teaches me that God expects me to use *all* of my gifts in
His service and challenges me to find a way to do so rather than
withdrawing from the exigencies of this earthly life.

I want to thank Sr. Mary Catharine Baseheart for her encouragement and her thoughtful foreword and Reverend John Sulli-
van for his generous help in preparing this new edition.

Waltraut Stein, Ph.D.
Atlanta, Georgia
October, 1988

Preface to the First and Second Editions

The translation of *Zum Problem der Einfühlung* presented here is a translation of the doctoral dissertation of Edith Stein, done under Edmund Husserl. The degree was awarded in 1916 at the University of Freiburg in Breisgau, and the dissertation in this form was published in 1917 at Halle.* The title of the treatise originally was *Das Einfühlungsproblem in seiner historischen Entwicklung und in phänomenologisher Betrachtung [The Empathy Problem as It Developed Historically and Considered Phenomenologically]*. The first historical chapter was omitted in publication and seems no longer to be extant.

This work is a description of the nature of empathy within the framework of Husserl's phenomenology as presented mainly in Volume I of *Ideas*. As Husserl's assistant, Edith had the opportunity to become intimately acquainted with his thinking. In fact, she edited Volume II of *Ideas* (cf. Husserliana IV, Martinus Nijhoff, 1952) which deals to a large extent with the same problems as her own work on empathy. Though she claims not to have seen Volume II before completing her own work (see *Author's Foreword*), she had evidently been following Husserl very closely as he was at that time working out his ideas. Thus her dissertation clearly shows how she has developed her interpretation of the

---

*A paperback reprint of the Halle edition was published by Gerhard Kaffke Verlag of München in 1980 (Edith-Stein-Karmel Tübingen, Edith Stein, *Zum Problem der Einfühlung*).

problem of empathy in terms of what Husserl later presented in this work left unpublished by him.

The significance of the work by E. Stein presented here also becomes evident when considered in relation to Maurice Merleau-Ponty's influential *Phénoménologie de la perception.*[1] Since Merleau-Ponty had access to the same unpublished manuscript of Volume II of *Ideas,* a number of his most important and interesting formulations take on a striking similarity to those of E. Stein. This is particularly true of the concept of the lived or living body (*Le Corps vécu or Leib*).

Many years after the completion of E. Stein's work on empathy, Husserl presented his *Cartesian Meditations* in French (1931), which is now also available in English (Martinus Nijhoff, 1960). In this work, however, Husserl is emphasizing a somewhat different aspect of the problem of empathy: the *possibility* of the other rather than the phenomenological *description* of this other. Thus *Cartesian Meditations* is more in contrast with his earlier conceptions than similar to them. This also means that E. Stein's work on empathy is in contrast with *Cartesian Meditations.* However, both E. Stein and Husserl adhere in all these works to the necessity for a phenomenological reduction to pure consciousness. Therefore, they can be considered works of phenomenology in the strict Husserlian sense.

The last third of E. Stein's chapter on "The Essence of Acts of Empathy" consists of a careful critique of Scheler's conception of empathy presented in his first edition of *Sympathiegefühle* (1913). Scheler considered Stein's analysis so pertinent that he referred to it three times in the second edition of this work (1923).[2]

This, then, is how *Zum Problem der Einfühlung* fits into the history of the phenomenological movement. On the other hand, the reader must not overlook that fact that E. Stein has made some original contributions to the phenomenological description of the nature of empathy. Some of these contributions, as the translator understands them, will be considered in the following introduction to the work.

At this time I want to acknowledge my indebtedness to Dr. James Sheridan, director of my master's thesis at Ohio University, in connection with which this translation was made. It is he who first led me to an understanding of the phenomenological position and the contents of E. Stein's work. Also Alfred Schuetz, Herbert Spiegelberg, William Earle, as well as my fellow graduate students at Northwestern University, have been most helpful by their suggestions, corrections, and encouragement. However, I myself assume full responsibility for any errors that may still remain in this translation.

Waltraut Stein, Ph.D.
1964

Translator's Introduction

The radical viewpoint of phenomenology is presented by
Edmund Husserl in his *Ideas*.[3] This viewpoint seems quite
simple at first, but becomes exceedingly complex and involves
intricate distinctions when attempts are made to apply it to actual
problems. Therefore, it may be well to attempt a short statement
of this position in order to note the general problems with which
it is dealing as well as the method of solution which it proposes. I
shall emphasize the elements of phenomenology which seem
most relevant to E. Stein's work.

Husserl deals with two traditional philosophical questions, and
in answering them, develops the method of phenomenological
reduction which he maintains is the basis of all science. These
questions are, "What is it that can be known without doubt?" and
"How is this knowledge possible in the most general sense?"

In the tradition of idealism he takes consciousness as the area to
be investigated. He posits *nothing* about the natural world. He
puts it in "brackets," as a portion of an algebraic formula is put in
brackets, and makes no use of the material within these brackets.
This does not mean that the "real" world does not exist, he says
emphatically; it only means that this existence is a presupposition
which must be suspended to achieve pure description.

It should be noted that the existence of most essences as well as
that of things or facts is suspended in this bracketing. Clear
knowledge of the existence of the idea of a thing transcendent to
consciousness is just as impossible as clear knowledge of the existence of natural objects, Husserl maintains.[4]

But what can possibly remain when things and essences have
been suspended? Husserl says that a realm of transcendental con-

sciousness remains, a consciousness which is in contrast with individual consciousness in the natural world. This transcendental or pure consciousness includes a subject, an act, and an object. Husserl emphasizes that consciousness is always active and always directed toward something. This active directedness he calls *intentionality*. The subject of consciousness is what wills, perceives, remembers, knows, evaluates, fantasizes. The act is the willing, perceiving, etc. The object, called "intentional object" or "phenomenon," is what is willed, perceived. In order to talk in this way, it is not necessary to state that the phenomenon exists anywhere but in consciousness. Furthermore, Husserl intends the designation "transcendental" to indicate that this consciousness is fundamental to any natural scientific effort because it prescribes what knowledge of the natural world must include. It is intersubjective in the same sense that natural science is. In other words, the phenomenologist's description of consciousness is verifiable by other people who are employing his method.

Husserl clearly is referring to Descartes' "Cogito, ergo sum" in stating that pure consciousness is what is known indubitably. The area of certain knowledge is that of consciousness.

It now becomes important not to confuse Husserl's "phenomenon" with the usual designation of phenomena as appearances or reflections from objects. Husserl has no such intentions. Pure consciousness is concerned with a realm of objects which are the same objects existing in the natural world. It only has a different "standpoint" in regard to them.

Answering the question of how knowledge is possible in the most general sense, Husserl maintains that a reduction to phenomena in an orderly manner is necessary. Phenomenologists must intuit the field of investigation so that the exact nature of the radical change from the natural standpoint and of the limits of the descriptive undertaking may become perfectly clear. Husserl calls this a methodological necessity and thus the reduction is called the phenomenological reduction. When this reduction has been made, the phenomenologist is in a position to intuit the essence or eidos of phenomena. Husserl calls this special kind of act *Wesenschauung* (intuition of essence).

E. Stein in the dissertation here presented takes the phenomenological standpoint. She claims that the description of empathy within consciousness after the suspension of the existence of empathy must be the basis for any other dealings with the problem by psychologists, sociologists, or biologists. The description she makes is a description of the pure transcendental phenomenon as it is observed from the special standpoint described above. It is impossible, she maintains as a phenomenologist, for the essence of empathy to be anything else if she has proceeded correctly. But it is still possible to describe the genesis of empathy in a real psycho-physical individual, the province of psychology.[5] The psychologist's work, however, only has validity insofar as he or she begins with and returns to the phenomenon which the phenomenologist has described. This is how phenomenology is the basis of psychology and at the same time how the analyses she has undertaken must be taken seriously by psychologists if they grant that pure description is fundamental to any other work.

This means that the significance of E. Stein's work lies in her descriptions of empathy, of the psycho-physical individual, and of the spiritual person. The descriptions of the psycho-physical individual and of the spiritual person are necessary in order to show the full implications and applications of the doctrine of empathy. This development takes place as follows.

In Chapter II E. Stein explains what it means to say that empathy is the givenness of foreign subjects and their experiences. She does this in terms of the pure "I," the subject of experience living in experience. Her conclusion is that empathy is not perception, representation nor a neutral positing, but *sui generis*.[6] It is an experience of being led by the foreign experience and takes place on three levels as follows:

1. The emergence of the experience;
2. The fulfilling explication;
3. The comprehensive objectification of the explained experience.[7]

This description makes it possible clearly to distinguish among empathy, sympathy, and a feeling of oneness.

Chapter III describes how the psycho-physical individual is

constituted within consciousness as sensed, living body and as outwardly perceived physical body. This constitution is unified by the phenomenon of fusion. The soul, an experience which is the basic bearer of all experiences, is founded on the body, and soul and body together form the psycho-physical individual.

In developing this conception of the psycho-physical individual, the author notes that sensations are among the real constituents of consciousness and cannot be bracketed.[8] These are absolutely given just as judging, willing, and perceiving. But there is a difference between sensations and these other acts. Sensations do not issue from the pure "I" and never take on the form of the *cogito* in which the "I" turns toward an object,[9] i.e., they are never aware of themselves. They are spatially localized somewhere at a distance from the "I" and these locations are always someplace in the living body.

On the contrary, the pure "I" cannot be localized. Nevertheless, my living body surrounds a "zero point of orientation" to which I relate my body and everything outside of it. Whatever refers to the "I" is given as at no distance from the zero point and everything given at a distance from the zero point is also given at a distance from the "I." An external thing can contact not me, but my physical body. Then its distance from my physical body but not from me becomes zero. Thus the living body as a whole is at the zero point while all physical bodies are outside of it.

This indicates that bodily space (of which the zero point is the "I") and outer space (of which the zero point is the living body) are very different. For instance, it cannot be said that the stone that I hold in my hand is the same distance or only a tiny bit farther from the zero point of orientation (i.e., from me) than the hand itself. In this case, the living body itself is the center of orientation and the stone is at a distance from it. This means that the distance of the parts of my living body from me is completely incomparable with the distance of foreign physical bodies from me.[10]

Let us consider for a moment the problem that this notion of a zero point of orientation seems to be intended to solve and whether this solution is acceptable. E. Stein hesitates to take the step from the constitution of the pure "I" to that of the physical, living body.[11] Why? The reason seems to be that she recognizes that she has the problem of showing how the pure "I" is related to the empirical "I" in a living body. This, it seems to me, is very close to the problem which Descartes also faced in trying to explain how an extended substance (matter) can be related to a non-extended substance (mind). Thus it appears that even though phenomenologists very possibly have solved the epistemological problem of how a knowing subject is related to the object of its knowledge by their concept of intentionality discussed above, they suddenly find themselves faced with the ontological problem of how an extended substance is related to a non-extended one.

Assuming, then, that this is the problem E. Stein faces at this point, let us examine her solution. She begins by maintaining that sensations are among the real constituents of consciousness, which means that they cannot be suspended or doubted any more than the cogito can. This, I believe, is a very exciting thesis that I have not found elaborated by other phenomenologists in this way. She seems to see these sensations as the bridge or link between the pure "I" and the living body. Let us see how this might be so. Sensations belong to the pure "I" because they cannot be suspended or bracketed. They therefore have one foot, so to speak, in the realm of pure consciousness, the realm of the non-extended in this discussion. On the other hand, sensations are always given as at some place in the living body, such as in the head for visual data or on the surface of the body for tactile data. In this way they participate in the realm of the extended, that of the physical body become a living body. Furthermore, sensations are always mine, giving further evidence that they belong to the "I."

But note that E. Stein must still maintain that sensations are spatially localized while the "I" is non-spatial. If it is meaningful to say that the "I" has sensations, however, and if sensations are always spatially localized, then it must be possible to say where the "I" is. She attempts to deal with this strange question by saying that "I" is at the "zero point of orientation" of the living body and has no distance from this, while any particular sensation is given at a distance from it. However, she adds that this zero point is at no particular place.[12] For purposes of outer perception, the living body itself serves as the zero point of orientation, and I see no reason to dispute this last observation.

However, it seems to me that further clarity must be gained on what it means to say that the "I" is at the zero point of orientation of the living body. Since this zero point is at no particular place, what does it mean to say that it is a point of orientation? What she wants to say, of course, is that the "I" is non-spatially localized, but what this means requires further elaboration. Until this has been clarified, it cannot be understood how the literally spatially localized sensations are at a distance from the non-spatially localized "I," and the problem of the relation of the extended to the non-extended cannot be considered as entirely resolved. However, this does not mean that this problem cannot be resolved by acknowledging sensations as real constituents of consciousness and given at places in the living body.

E. Stein continues her analysis by noting that the living body is constituted in a two-fold manner: (1) as sensed or bodily perceived living body [*Leib*] and (2) as outwardly perceived physical body [*Körper*] of the outer world.[13] It is experienced as the same in this double givenness. By bodily perception she means the perception of my body from the inside as distinguished from outer perception or sensations of objects. But she does not fail to note that sensations of objects are given at the living body to the living body as senser,[14] and so they are intimately connected with bodily perception. She calls this double mode of experiencing objects the phenomenon of "fusion": I see the hand and what it senses or touches and also bodily perceive this hand touching this object.

Furthermore, this psycho-physical individual only becomes aware of its living body as a physical body like others when it empathically realizes that its own zero point of orientation is a spatial point among many. Thus, it is first given to itself in the full sense in reiterated empathy.[15]

In her description of the spiritual person in Chapter IV, E. Stein shows how the spirit differs from the soul. The soul, as a part of nature, is subject to natural causality. The spirit, which faces the natural world, is subject to a meaning context based on motivation. She describes motivation as the symbolic, experienced proceeding of one experience from another without a detour over the object sphere.[16] She develops this conception of the spiritual person in terms of feelings which are the necessary basis for volition and ground valuing. The description of feelings reveals an "I" with various depths or levels. This is, of course, not the pure "I" of Chapter II. With the additional consideration of intensity and spread, a hierarchy of value feelings can be established and a doctrine of types of persons developed. On the basis of these complex relationships among feelings, volitions, and values revealing types, the spiritual person becomes intelligible. E. Stein then observes that we become aware of levels of value in ourselves by empathizing with persons of our own type. By becoming aware, also by empathy, that there are persons of types different from ours, we see that certain ranges of value are closed to us.

There seems to be an assumption in this discussion of the spiritual person that, while probably following Husserl and Scheler, nevertheless seems to be unjustified. This is the contention that values and feelings have a rationality no different from logical rationality. The experienced proceeding of one experience from another forms meaning contexts, E. Stein says. These contexts indicate an *a priori* rational lawfulness in values, volition, and action like that in logic.[17] She develops this notion with the implication that the person can, in principle, be understood completely in terms of various depths of values and feelings which form themselves into personal types.

This makes the intelligibility of the spiritual person parallel to the intelligibility of the physical individual understood in terms of mechanical causality. She seems, then, to be assuming that when a person violates this rational lawfulness of values and feelings, this person's behavior is necessarily irrational and incomprehensible. But it seems that, just because some feelings and values are deeper than others and we actually expect certain kinds of behavior from individuals of certain types, it does not at all follow that the person who violates these expectations and levels is necessarily irrational in a strictly logical sense. It is true that such a person's behavior does not make sense to us now, but may this not be the fault of the types and the depth hierarchy we have described? If this approach to understanding spiritual persons is to be useful, we must continually revise our classifications as new phenomena present themselves, rather than dismiss some forms of behavior as "irrational." To dismiss behavior in this way is actually to abdicate a readiness to understand.

E. Stein is certainly to be credited here with seeing that mechanical causation as an explanation of physical phenomena is not appropriate for explaining spiritual phenomena, and the interpretative scheme she proposes is very interesting. But it seems that such a scheme must be left open and distinguished from logical rationality rather than identified with it.

In this work E. Stein has thus shown what empathy is and how it is important in understanding our own nature as well as that of others. She has done an admirable job of analyzing and describing the various aspects and presentations of the phenomenon of empathy within the framework of the phenomenological method. Her approach is clear and direct and her examples are apt. She also makes distinctions with a fineness of perception that is truly remarkable.

A final possible value of this work may lie in an insight which E. Stein has in common with Sigmund Freud but has apparently arrived at independently. She shows that an experience which took place in the past can exist in the background of present experience and still have an effect.[18] She calls this mode of existence the mode of non-actuality. Freud in his analysis of personality says that an experience may be repressed by the superego but continue to exist in the id. At a later time, if the superego is weakened, the repressed experience may break out of the id and affect the behavior of the ego. The mode of existence of material in the id Freud calls unconscious. A synthesis of the views of non-actuality and unconscious, one of which was arrived at by the method of phenomenology and the other by an architectonic of the person in a naturalistic context, might be both profitable and interesting.

Waltraut Stein, Ph.D.
1962

Notes on the Translation

The pagination of the original has been retained in the left-hand margin and all footnotes and cross references refer to these pages.

In general, W.R.B. Gibson's translation of the *Ideen*[19] has been followed for the translation of technical phenomenological terminology. An exception is *Ausschaltung*, which has been rendered "exclusion" rather than "disconnection."

In Chapter III the distinction between *Körper* and *Leib* becomes very important. While this distinction is quite clear in German, the usual translation in English is "body" for both words. *Körper* signifies the material or physical aspects of one's body, i.e., that which can be sensually perceived as matter. By contrast, *Leib* emphasizes the animation of the body, the perception of it as alive instead of simply as a thing. In accordance with this distinction the word *Körper* has usually been rendered as "physical body" and *Leib* as "living body."

The distinction between *Erlebnis* and *Erfahrung* becomes important in several places. E. Stein used *Erlebnis* in the most general sense of experience, i.e., as anything which happens to a subject. In the few places where she uses *Erfahrung*, she is emphasizing sense experience, such as the experience or perception of foreign experience. To make this distinction clear, *Erfahrung* has been rendered as "perception" or "perceiving," with the German in brackets to distinguish it from *Wahrnehmung*. *Erlebnis* has consistently been translated as "experience."

The word *hineinversetzen* also has no simple English equivalent. Literally it refers to the act of transferring or putting oneself into another's place. "Projection into" seemed to be the most satisfactory translation.

A further problem arose with the translation of *Seele* and *seelisch*. *Seele* most clearly means "soul" in the sense of psyche and has been rendered as such. However, "soulful" or "spiritual" in English does not render the sense of *seelisch*. As far as the translator could see, E. Stein is not making a distinction between *seelisch* and *psychisch* and so both words have been rendered as "psychic."

The translation of *Geist* in Chapter IV presented a special problem, since neither of the two usual renderings into English, "mind" or "spirit," is really satisfactory. The connotations of "mind" are too narrow, while those of "spirit" are too broad. "Spirit" has been selected for this third edition with the caveat that the reader keep in mind that the author is not referring to a moral or religious entity in this context. Rather, the sense is of the creative human spirit that is the subject matter of what we call the humanities, the social sciences, and law and that the Germans call *Geisteswissenschaften*, literally "investigations into spirit." *Geisteswissenschaften* has been translated as "cultural sciences," a common rendering of this term.

ON THE PROBLEM OF EMPATHY

Foreword

T he complete work, from which the following expositions <V>
are taken, began with a purely historical treatment of the
problems emerging one by one in the literature on empathy
before me: aesthetic empathy, empathy as the cognitive source of
foreign [*fremdes*] experience, ethical empathy, etc. Though I
found these problems mingled together, I separated them in my
presentation. Moreover, the epistemological, purely descriptive,
and genetic-psychological aspects of this identified problem were
undistinguished from one another. This mingling showed me
why no one has found a satisfactory solution so far.

Above all, it seemed that I should extract the basic problem so
that all the others would become intelligible from its viewpoint.
And I wanted to submit this problem to a basic investigation. At
the same time, it seemed to me that this positive work was a
requisite foundation for criticizing the prevailing conclusions. I
recognized this basic problem to be the question of empathy as
the perceiving [*Erfahrung*] of foreign subjects and their experience [*Erleben*]. The following expositions will deal with this question.

I am very well aware that my positive results represent only a
very small contribution to what is to be realized. In addition,
special circumstances have prevented me from once more thor- <VI>
oughly revising the work before publication. Since I submitted it
to the faculty, I have, in my capacity as private assistant to my

1

respected Professor Husserl, had a look at the manuscript of Part II of his "Ideen," dealing in part with the same question. Thus, naturally, should I take up my theme again, I would not be able to refrain from using the new suggestions received. Of course, the statement of the problem and my method of work have grown entirely out of intellectual stimuli received from Professor Husserl so that in any case what I may claim as my "spiritual property" in the following expositions is most questionable. Nevertheless, I can say that the results I now submit have been obtained by my own efforts. This I could no longer maintain if I now undertook changes.

Chapter II

The Essence of Acts of Empathy

1. The Method of the Investigation

All controversy over empathy is based on the implied as-   <1>
sumption that foreign subjects and their experience are
given to us. Thinkers deal with the circumstances of the occurrence, the effects, and the legitimacy of this givenness. But the
most immediate undertaking is to consider the phenomenon of
givenness in and by itself and to investigate its essence. We shall
do this in the setting of the "phenomenological reduction."

The goal of phenomenology is to clarify and thereby to find the
ultimate basis of all knowledge. To reach this goal it considers
nothing that is in any way "doubtful," nothing that can be elimi-
nated. In the first place, it does not use any results of science
whatsoever. This is self-evident, for a science which proposes
ultimately to clarify all scientific knowledge must not, in turn, be
based on a science already extant, but must be grounded in itself.

Is it based on natural experience then? By no means, for even
this as well as its continuation, research in natural science, is
subject to diverse interpretations (as in materialistic or idealistic
philosophy) and thus stands in need of clarification. Therefore,
the entire surrounding world, the physical as well as the psycho-
physical, the bodies as well as the souls of men and animals (including the psycho-physical person of the investigator himself) is
subject to the exclusion or reduction.

What can be left if the whole world and even the subject experiencing it are cancelled? In fact, there remains an infinite field of <2> pure investigation. For let us consider what this exclusion means. I can doubt whether what I see before me exists. Deception is possible. Therefore, I must exclude and make no use of the positing of existence. But what I cannot exclude, what is not subject to doubt, is my experience of the thing (the perception, memory, or other kind of comprehension) together with its correlate, the full "phenomenon of the thing" (the object given as the same in series of diverse perceptions or memories). This phenomenon retains its entire character and can be made into an object of consideration. (There are difficulties in seeing how it is possible to suspend the positing of existence and still retain the full character of perception. The case of hallucination illustrates this possibility. Let us suppose that someone suffers from hallucinations and has insight into his condition. In a room with a healthy person, he may suppose that he sees a door in the wall and want to go through it. When his attention is called to this, he realizes that he is hallucinating again. Now he no longer believes that the door is present, even being able to transfer himself into the "cancelled" perception. This offers him an excellent opportunity for studying the nature of perception, including the positing of existence, even though he no longer participates in this.)

Thus there remains the whole "phenomenon of the world" when its positing has been suspended. And these "phenomena" are the object of phenomenology. However, it is not sufficient merely to comprehend them individually and to explain what is implied in them, inquiring into the tendencies enclosed in the simple having of the phenomenon. Rather, we must press forward to their essence. Each phenomenon forms an exemplary basis for the consideration of essence. The phenomenology of perception, not satisfied with describing the single perception, wants to ascertain what "perception is essentially as such." It acquires this knowledge from the single case in ideational abstraction.[20]

<3> We must still show what it means to say that my experience is not to be excluded. It is not indubitable that I exist, this empirical "I" of this name and station, given such and such attributes. My

whole past could be dreamed or be a deceptive recollection. Therefore, it is subject to the exclusion, only remaining an object of consideration as a phenomenon. But "I," the experiencing subject who considers the world and my own person as phenomenon, "I" am in experience and only in it, am just as indubitable and impossible to cancel as experience itself.

Now let us apply this way of thinking to our case. The world in which we live is not only a world of physical bodies but also of experiencing subjects external to us, of whose experiences we know. This knowledge is not indubitable. Precisely here we are subject to such diverse deceptions that occasionally we are inclined to doubt the possibility of knowledge in this domain at all. But the phenomenon of foreign psychic life is indubitably there, and we now want to examine this a little further.

However, the direction of the investigation is not yet clearly prescribed. We could proceed from the complete, concrete phenomenon before us in our experiential world, the phenomenon of a psycho-physical individual which is clearly distinguished from a physical thing. This individual is not given as a physical body, but as a sensitive, living body belonging to an "I," an "I" that senses, thinks, feels, and wills. The living body of this "I" not only fits into my phenomenal world but is itself the center of orientation of such a phenomenal world. It faces this world and communicates with me.

And we could investigate how whatever appears to us beyond the mere physical body given in outer perception is constituted within consciousness.

Moreover, we could consider the single, concrete experiences of these individuals. Different ways of being given would then <4> appear, and we could further pursue these. It would become apparent that there are other ways of being given "in the symbolic relation" than the givenness worked out by Lipps. I not only know what is expressed in facial expressions and gestures, but also what is hidden behind them. Perhaps I see that someone makes a sad face but is not really sad. I may also hear someone make an indiscreet remark and blush. Then I not only understand the remark and see shame in the blush, but I also discern that he knows his remark is indiscreet and is ashamed of himself for having made it. Neither this motivation nor the judgment about his remark is expressed by any "sensory appearance."

This investigation will be concerned with these various ways of being given and possibly with the underlying relationships present. But a still more radical examination is possible. All these data of foreign experience point back to the basic nature of acts in which foreign experience is comprehended. We now want to designate these acts as empathy, regardless of all historical traditions attached to the word. To grasp and describe these acts in the greatest essential generality will be our first undertaking.

2. Description of Empathy in Comparison With Other Acts

We shall be able to see emphatic acts best in their individuality if we confront them with other acts of pure consciousness (our field of consideration after making the described reduction). Let us take an example to illustrate the nature of the act of empathy. A friend tells me that he has lost his brother and I become aware of his pain. What kind of an awareness is this? I am not concerned here with going into the basis on which I infer the pain. Perhaps his face is pale and disturbed, his voice toneless and strained. Perhaps he also expresses his pain in words. Naturally, these things can all be investigated, but they are not my concern here. I would like to know, not how I arrive at this awareness, but what it itself is.

<5>

(a) Outer Perception and Empathy

Needless to say, I have no outer perception of the pain. Outer perception is a term for acts in which spatio-temporal concrete being and occurring come to me in embodied givenness. This being has the quality of being there itself right now; it turns this or that side to me and the side turned to me is embodied in a specific sense. It is primordially there in comparison with sides co-perceived but averted.

The pain is not a thing and is not given to me as a thing, even when I am aware of it "in" the pained countenance. I perceive this countenance outwardly and the pain is given "at one" with it.

There is a close, yet very loose, parallel between empathic acts and the averted sides of what is seen, because in progressive perception I can always bring new sides of the thing to primordial givenness. Each side can, in principle, assume this primordial givenness I select. I can consider the expression of pain, more accurately, the change of face I empathically grasp as an expression of pain, from as many sides as I desire. Yet, in principle, I can never get an "orientation" where the pain itself is primordially given.

Thus empathy does not have the character of outer perception, though it does have something in common with outer perception: In both cases the object itself is present here and now. We have come to recognize outer perception as an act given primordially. But, though empathy is not outer perception, this is not to say that it does not have this "primordiality."   <6>

(b) Primordiality and Non-primordiality

There are things other than the outer world given to us primordially; for instance, there is ideation which is the intuitive comprehension of essential states. Insight into a geometric axiom is primordially given as well as valuing. Finally and above all, our own experiences as they are given in reflection have the character of primordiality.

Since empathy deals with grasping what is here and now, it is trivial to say that it is not ideation. (Whether it can serve as a basis for ideation, which is the attainment of an essential knowledge of experiences, is another question.)

Now there is still the question of whether empathy has the primordiality of our own experience. Before we can answer this question, we must further differentiate the meaning of primordiality. All our own present experiences are primordial. What could be more primordial than experience itself?[21]

But not all experiences are primordially given nor primordial in their content. Memory, expectation, and fantasy do not have their object bodily present before them. They only represent it, and this character of representation is an immanent, essential moment of these acts, not a sign from their objects.

Finally, there is the question of the givenness of our own experiences themselves. It is possible for every experience to be primordially given, i.e., it is possible for the reflecting glance of the "I" in the experience to be there bodily itself. Furthermore, it is possible for our own experiences to be given non-primordially in memory, expectation, or fantasy.

Now we again take up the question of whether empathy is primordial and in what sense.

(c) Memory, Expectation, Fantasy, and Empathy

There is a well-known analogy between acts of empathy and acts in which our own experiences are given non-primordially. <7> The memory of a joy is primordial as a representational act now being carried out, though its content of joy is non-primordial. This act has the total character of joy which I could study, but the joy is not primordially and bodily there, rather as having once been alive (and this "once," the time of the past experience, can be definite or indefinite). The present non-primordiality points back to the past primordiality. This past has the character of a former "now." Accordingly, memory posits, and what is remembered has being.

Further, there are two possibilities: The "I" as the subject of the act of remembering, in this act of representation, can look back at the past joy. Then the past joy is the intentional object of the "I," its subject being with and in the "I" of the past. Thus the present "I" and the past "I" face each other as subject and object. They do not coincide, though there is a consciousness of sameness. But this is not a positive identification and, moreover, the distinction between the primordially remembering "I" and the "I" non-primordially remembered persists. Memory can also be accomplished in other modes. The same act of representation in which what is remembered emerges before me as a whole implies certain tendencies. When these unfold, they expose "traits" in their temporal course, how the whole remembered experience was once primordially constituted.[22]

This process can occur passively "in me" or I can do it actively step by step. I can even carry out the passive, as well as the active, course of memory without reflecting, without having the present "I," the subject of the act of memory, before me in any way. Or I can expressly set myself back to that time in a continuous stream

of experiences, allowing the past experiential sequence to re-
awaken, living in the remembered experience instead of turning   <8>
to it as an object. However, the memory always remains a representation with a non-primordial subject which is in contrast with
the subject doing the remembering. The reproduction of the
former experience is the clarification of what was vaguely intended at first.

At the end of the process there is a new objectification. I now
unite the past experience, which first arose before me as a whole
and which I then took apart while projecting myself into it, in an
"apperceptive grip." Diverse forms of memory can have a variety
of gaps. Thus it is possible for me to represent a past situation to
myself and be unable to remember my inner behavior in this
situation. As I transfer myself back into this situation, a surrogate
for the missing memory comes into focus. This image of the past
behavior is not, however, a representation of what is past. Rather,
it is the requisite completion of the memory image to get the
meaning of the whole. It can have the character of doubt, conjec-
ture, or possibility, but never the character of being.

It is hardly necessary to go into the case of expectation, since it
is so parallel. But something can still be said about free fantasy.
Fantasy, too, can be accomplished in various ways: An experience
of fantasy can arise as a whole and the tendencies implied in it
fulfilled step by step. In fantasy there is no temporal distance,
filled by continuous experiences, between the fantasizing and the
fantasized "I," provided I do not just happen to be dealing with a
fantasized memory or expectation.

But there is also a distinction here. The "I" producing the
fantasized world is primordial; the "I" living in it is non-primordial. The fantasized experiences are in contrast with memory
because they are not given as a representation of actual experiences but as the non-primordial form of present experiences.
This "present" does not indicate a present of objective time but
an experienced present which in this case can only be objectified
in a "neutral"[23] present of fantasized time. The neutralized or   <9>
non-posited form of the present memory (the representation of a
givenness now real but not possessing a body) is in contrast with a
neutralized pre- and post-memory. That is to say, it is in contrast

with a fantasy of the past and of the future, with the representation of unreal past and future experiences. It is also possible for me to meet myself in the realm of fantasy (as well as in memory or expectation), i.e., to meet an "I" which I recognize as myself though there is no linking continuity of experience to establish the unity, so to speak, to meet my mirror image. (This reminds us, for example, of the experience Goethe relates in *Dichtung und Wahrheit*. One evening he was coming from Sesenheim after saying good-bye to Friederike, and he met himself on the way in his future form.) But this does not seem to be the genuine fantasy of our own experiences. Rather, it seems to be an analogue to empathy which can be understood only from the viewpoint of empathy.

So now to empathy itself. Here, too, we are dealing with an act which is primordial as present experience though non-primordial in content. And this content is an experience which, again, can be had in different ways such as in memory, expectation, or in fantasy. When it arises before me all at once, it faces me as an object (such as the sadness I "read in another's face"). But when I inquire into its implied tendencies (try to bring another's mood to clear givenness to myself), the content, having pulled me into it, is no longer really an object. I am now no longer turned to the content but to the object of it, am at the subject of the content in the original subject's place. And only after successfully executed clarification, does the content again face me as an object.[24]

<10>   Thus in all the cases of the representation of experiences considered, there are three levels or modalities of accomplishment even if in a concrete case people do not always go through all levels but are often satisfied with one of the lower ones. These are (1) the emergence of the experience, (2) the fulfilling explication, and (3) the comprehensive objectification of the explained experience. On the first and third levels, the representation exhibits the non-primordial parallel to perception, and on the second level it exhibits the non-primordial parallel to the having of the experience. The subject of the empathized experience, however, is not the subject empathizing, but another. And this is what is fundamentally new in contrast with the memory, expectation, or the fantasy of our own experiences. These two subjects are sepa-

rate and not joined together, as previously, by a consciousness of sameness or a continuity of experience. And while I am living in the other's joy, I do not feel primordial joy. It does not issue live from my "I." Neither does it have the character of once having lived like remembered joy. But still much less is it merely fantasized without actual life. This other subject is primordial although I do not experience it as primordial. In my non-primordial experience I feel, as it were, led by a primordial one not experienced by me but still there, manifesting itself in my non-primordial experience.

Thus empathy is a kind of act of perceiving [*eine Art erfahrender Akte*] *sui generis*. We have set ourselves the task of expounding it in its peculiarity before tackling any other question (of whether such experience is valid or how it occurs). And we have conducted this investigation in purest generality. Empathy, which we examined and sought to describe, is the experience of foreign consciousness in general, irrespective of the kind of the experiencing subject or of the subject whose consciousness is experienced. We only discussed the pure "I," the subject of experience, on the subject's as well as on the object's side. Nothing else was drawn into the investigation.

The experience which an "I" as such has of another "I" as such looks like this. This is how human beings comprehend the psychic life of their fellows. Also as believers they comprehend the love, the anger, and the precepts of their God in this way; and God can comprehend people's lives in no other way. As the possessor of complete knowledge, God is not mistaken about people's experiences, as people are mistaken about each others' experiences. But people's experiences do not become God's own, either; nor do they have the same kind of givenness for Him.

3. Discussion in Terms of Other Descriptions of Empathy— Especially That of [T.] Lipps—and Continuation of the Analysis

Naturally, this general presentation of the nature of "empathy on the whole" does not accomplish much. We must now investigate how empathy is differentiated as the perception of psycho-

physical individuals and their experience of personality, etc. Yet
from the conclusions already reached, it is possible to criticize
some historical theories of how foreign consciousness is experienced. By means of this criticism, we can also complete our analysis along some lines.

Lipps' description of the experience of empathy agrees with
ours in many respects. (We shall not deal with his causal-genetic
hypothesis of the circumstances of empathy, the theory of inner
imitation, because he mixes it almost entirely with pure description.) To be sure, he does not conduct his investigation in pure
generality, sticking to the case of the psycho-physical individual
and to "symbolic givenness," but we can still generalize in part
the conclusions he reaches.

(a) Points of Agreement

Lipps depicts empathy as an "inner participation" in foreign
experiences. Doubtless, this is equivalent to our highest level of
the consummation of empathy—where we are "at" the foreign
subject and turned with it to its object. He stresses the objectivity
or the "demanding" character of empathy and thus expresses
what we mean by designating it as a kind of act undergone.
Further, he indicates how empathy is akin to memory and expectation. But this brings us directly to a point where our ways part.

<12>

(b) The Tendency to Full Experiencing

Lipps speaks of the fact that every experience about which I
know, including those remembered and expected as well as those
empathized, "tends" to be fully experienced. And it is fully experienced if nothing in me opposes it. At the same time the "I,"
an object until now, is experienced. This is so whether the "I" is
past or future, my own or the foreign "I." He also calls this full
experiencing of foreign experience empathy. Indeed, he first sees
full empathy here, the other being an incomplete, preliminary
level of empathy.

That the subject of the remembered, expected, or empathized
experience in this second form of memory, expectation, or empathy is not properly an object is in agreement with our conception.
But we do not agree that there is a complete coincidence with the

remembered, expected, or empathized "I," that they become one. Lipps confuses the following two acts: (1) being drawn into the experience at first given objectively and fulfilling its implied tendencies with (2) the transition from non-primordial to primordial experience.

A memory is entirely fulfilled and identified when one has followed out all its tendencies to explication and established the experiential continuity to the present. But this does not make the remembered experience primordial. The present viewpoint of the remembered state of affairs is completely independent of the remembered viewpoint. I can remember a perception and now be convinced that I was formerly under a delusion. I remember my discomfort in an embarrassing situation and now think it was very funny. In this case the memory is no more incomplete than if I again take the former viewpoint.

We agree that a shift from remembered, expected or empathized to primordial experience is possible. But we do not agree that, when this tendency has been fulfilled, memory, expectation, or empathy is still present.   <13>

Let us consider the case further. I actively bring to mind a former joy, for example, of a passed examination. I transfer myself into it, i.e., I turn to the joyful event and depict it to myself in all its joyfulness. Suddenly I notice that I, this primordial, remembering "I," am full of joy. I remember the joyful event and take primordial joy in the remembered event. However, the memory joy and the memory "I" have vanished or, at most, persist beside the primordial joy and the primordial "I." Naturally, this primordial joy over past events can also occur directly. This would be a mere representation of the event without my remembering the former joy or making a transition from the remembered to the primordial event. Finally, I may be primordially joyful over the past joy, making the difference between these two acts especially prominent.

Now let us take the parallel to empathy. My friend comes to me beaming with joy and tells me he has passed his examination. I comprehend his joy empathically; transferring myself into it, I comprehend the joyfulness of the event and am now primordially joyful over it myself. I can also be joyful without first compre-

hending the joy of the other. Should the examination candidate step into the tense, impatient family circle and impart the joyful news, in the first place, they will be primordially joyful over this news. Only when they have been "joyful long enough" themselves, will they be joyful over their joy or, perhaps as the third possibility, be joyful over his joy.[25] But his joy is neither given to us as primordial joy over the event nor as primordial joy over his joy. Rather it is given as this non-primordial act of empathy that
<14>   we have already described more precisely.

On the other hand, if, as in memory, we put ourselves in the place of the foreign "I" and suppress it while we surround ourselves with its situation, we have one of these situations of "appropriate" experience. If we then again concede to the foreign "I" its place and ascribe this experience to him, we gain a knowledge of his experience. (According to Adam Smith, this is how foreign experience is given.) Should empathy fail, this procedure can make up the deficiency, but it is not itself an experience. We could call this surrogate for empathy an "assumption" but not empathy itself, as [A.] Meinong does.[26] Empathy in our strictly defined sense as the experience of foreign consciousness can only be the non-primordial experience which announces a primordial one. It is neither the primordial experience nor the "assumed" one.

(c) Empathy and Fellow Feeling

Should empathy persist beside primordial joy over the joyful event (beside the comprehension of the joy of the other), and, moreover, should the other really be conscious of the event as joyful (possibly it is also joyful for me, for example, if this passed examination is the condition for a trip together so that I am happy for him as the means to it), we can designate this primordial act as joy-with-him or, more generally, as fellow feeling (*sympathy*).[27] Sympathized and empathized joy need not necessarily be the same in content at all. (They are certainly not the same in respect to quality, since one is a primordial and the other a non-primordial experience.) The joy of the most intimate participant will generally be more intense and enduring than the others' joy.
<15>   But it is also possible for the others' joy to be more intense. They

may be naturally capable of more intense feelings than he; they may be "altruistic" and "values for others" *eo ipso* mean more to them than "values for themselves"; finally, this event may have lost some of its value through circumstances unknown to the others. On the other hand, in the ideal case (where there is no deception) empathic joy expressly claims to be the same in every respect as comprehended joy, to have the same content and only a different mode of being given.

(d) Negative Empathy

Lipps has called the primordial experience that can be added to the experience of empathy full, positive empathy. With this he has contrasted a negative empathy: the case in which the tendency of the empathic experience to become a primordial experience of my own cannot be realized because "something in me" opposes it. This may be either a momentary experience of my own or my kind of personality.

We also want to investigate this further, again, in pure generality. The "personality" has transcendencies as well as a qualitatively developed present "I," which are themselves subject to exclusion and are only considered by us as phenomena. Let us take the following case. I am completely filled with grief over a bereavement at the moment my friend tells me the joyful news. This grief does not permit the predominance of sympathy with the joy. There is a conflict (again, not real but phenomenal) involving two levels. The "I" living entirely in the grief perhaps at first experiences empathy as a "background experience." This is comparable to peripheral areas of the visual field that are seen and yet are not intentional objects in the full sense, are not objects of actual attention. And now the "I" feels pulled toward two sides at once, both experiences claiming to be a "cogito" in a specific sense (i.e., acts in which the "I" lives and turns toward its object). Both seek to pull the "cogito" into themselves. This is precisely the experience of being split. Thus on the first level there is a split between our own actual experience and the empathic experience. It is further possible for the "I" to be pulled into the empathic <16> experience, to turn to the other's joyful object. At the same time, this other pull may not cease so that an actual joy can prevail.

But it seems to me that in neither case is it a question of a specific trait of in- or with-feeling (*empathy or sympathy*), but of one of the typical forms of transition from one "cogito" to another in general. There are numerous such transitions: A cogito can be completely lived out so that I can then "entirely spontaneously" flow over into another one. Further, while I am living in one cogito, another can appear and pull me into it without causing conflict. Finally, the tendencies implied in the cogito and not yet entirely consummated can obstruct the transition to a new cogito. And all this is just as possible in perception, memory, in theoretical contemplation, etc. as in empathy.

(e) Empathy and a Feeling of Oneness

I would also like to examine a little more closely this unity of our own and the foreign "I" in empathy that was earlier rejected. Lipps says that as long as empathy is complete (exactly what we no longer recognize as empathy) there is no distinction between our own and the foreign "I," that they are one. For example, I am one with the acrobat and go through his motions inwardly. A distinction only arises when I step out of complete empathy and reflect on my "real 'I'." Then the experiences not coming from me appear to belong to "the other" and to lie in his movements. Were this description correct, the distinction between foreign and our own experiences, as well as that between the foreign and our own "I," would actually be suspended. This distinction would first occur in association with various "real 'I's' " or psycho-physical individuals. What my body is doing to my body and what the foreign body is doing to the foreign body would then remain completely obscure, since I am living "in" the one in the same way as in the other, experience the movements of the one in the same way as those of the other.

<17>   This assertion is not only refuted by its consequences, but is also an evidently false description. I am not one with the acrobat but only "at" him. I do not actually go through his motions but *quasi*. Lipps also stresses, to be sure, that I do not outwardly go through his motions. But neither is what "inwardly" corresponds to the movements of the body, the experience that "I move," primordial; it is non-primordial for me. And in these non-primor-

dial movements I feel led, accompanied, by his movements. Their primordiality is declared in my non-primordial movements which are only there for me in him (again understood as experienced, since the pure bodily movement is also perceived outwardly). Every movement the spectator makes is primordial. For example, he may pick up his dropped program and not "know" it because he is living entirely in empathy. But should he reflect in the one instance as in the other (for which it is necessary for his "I" to carry out the transition from one cogito to the other), he would find in one instance a primordial and in the other a non-primordial givenness. And this non-primordiality is not simple but is a non-primordiality in which foreign primordiality becomes apparent. What led Lipps astray in his description was the confusion of self-forgetfulness, through which I can surrender myself to any object, with a dissolution of the "I" in the object. Thus, strictly speaking, empathy is not a feeling of oneness.

But this does not mean that there is no such thing as a feeling of oneness. Let us go back to sympathy with foreign experience. We said that the "I" in co-experiencing another is turned toward the object of the foreign experience, that it has the foreign experience present empathically at the same time, and that the sympathetic and empathic act do not have to coincide in content. Now let us modify this case somewhat. A special edition of the paper reports that the fortress has fallen. As we hear this, all of us are seized by an excitement, a joy, a jubilation. We all have "the same" feeling. Have thus the barriers separating one "I" from another broken down here? Has the "I" been freed from its   <18> monadic character? Not entirely. I feel my joy while I empathically comprehend the others' and see it as the same. And, seeing this, it seems that the non-primordial character of the foreign joy has vanished. Indeed, this phantom joy coincides in every respect with my real live joy, and theirs is just as live to them as mine is to me. Now I intuitively have before me what they feel. It comes to life in my feeling, and from the "I" and "you" arises the "we" as a subject of a higher level.[28]

And it is also possible for us to be joyful over the same event, though not filled with exactly the same joy. Joyfulness may be more richly accessible to the others, which difference I comprehend empathically. I empathically arrive at the "sides" of joyful-ness obstructed in my own joy. This ignites my joy, and only now is there complete coincidence with what is empathized. If the same thing happens to the others, we empathically enrich our feeling so that "we" now feel a different joy from "I," "you," and "he" in isolation. But "I," "you," and "he" are retained in "we." A "we," not an "I," is the subject of the empathizing. Not through the feeling of oneness, but through empathizing, do we experience others. The feeling of oneness and the enrichment of our own experience become possible through empathy.

(f) Reiteration of Empathy—Reflexive Sympathy

I would like to call attention to just one more concept from Lipps' description: that which he designates as "reflexive sympa-thy" and which I would like to call the reiteration of empathy, more exactly, a particular case of reiteration.

Empathy has this attribute in common with many kinds of acts. There is not only reflection, but also reflection on reflection, etc. <19> as an ideal possibility *ad infinitum*. Similarly, there is a willing of willing, a liking of liking, etc. In fact, all representations can be reiterated. I can remember a memory, expect an expectation, fantasy a fantasy. And so I can also empathize the empathized, i.e., among the acts of another that I comprehend empathically there can be empathic acts in which the other comprehends an-other's acts. This "other" can be a third person or me myself. In the second case we have "reflexive sympathy" where my original experience returns to me as an empathized one. The significance of this phenomenon in the give and take between individuals does not need to concern us here because we are only dealing with the general essence of empathy and not with its effect.

4. The Controversy Between the View of Idea and That of Actuality

Perhaps from the viewpoint of our description of empathic acts, we can find access to the much-discussed question of whether empathy has the character of an idea [*Vorstellung*] or of actuality. [M.] Geiger has already stressed that this question is equivocal and that various points must be distinguished:[29] (1) Are empathized experiences primordial or not? (2) Are foreign experiences objectively given as something facing me or given experientially? (3) Are they intuitively or non-intuitively given (and if intuitively, in the character of perception or of representation)?

After the preceding discussion, we can flatly answer the first question in the negative. But we cannot so easily answer the second question in terms of our presentation. There is a two-sidedness to the essence of empathic acts: an experience of our own announcing another one. And there are various levels of accomplishment possible. For instance, we may turn toward the foreign experience and feel ourselves led by it. Or empathic explication may lead us to realize what was first vaguely meant. In the second case, one cannot speak of objectivity in a pregnant <20> sense, even though the foreign experience certainly "is there" for me.

The third question likewise requires further investigation. We have already seen what distinguishes empathy from perception and what they have in common. Perception has its object before it in embodied givenness; empathy does not. But both have their object itself there and meet it directly where it is anchored in the continuity of being. They need not represent it in order to draw it close. Mere knowledge [*Wissen*] is also characterized by this "encountering" by the subject, but is created in this encounter. It is nothing more. Knowledge reaches its object but does not "have" it. It stands before its object but does not see it. Knowledge is blind, empty, and restless, always pointing back to some kind of experienced, seen act. And the experience back to which knowledge of foreign experience points is called empathy. I know of another's grief, i.e., either I have comprehended this grief empathically but am no longer in the "intuiting" act, content with empty knowledge, or I know of this grief on the basis of a communication. Then the grief is not given to me intuitively, though surely to the communicator. (Should this be the griever himself, it is primordially given to him in reflection. Should it be a third person, he comprehends it non-primordially in empathy.)

And from his experience I once more have an experience, i.e., I comprehend the grief empathically. A further analysis of the relationship of "empathy" to "knowledge of foreign experience" is not required at this point. It is enough that we have reciprocally limited them.

The conclusion from our discussion is that the original controversial question was badly put. Thus no answer to it could be correct. For example, Witasek, a particularly energetic defender of the view of idea,[30] does not take our distinctions into consideration at all. He takes the objective character of empathy to be <21> proved along with its representational character. By a further equivocation of idea (which is an intellectual experience in contrast with an emotional one), he arrives at the absurd consequence of denying that empathized feelings involve emotion. He even bases his conclusion on a special argument: Empathy cannot involve feelings because the "assumption of feeling" is missing (the "something" to which feeling could be related). The empathizing subject would only assume feeling in the subject having the feelings if he were dealing with a projection [*Hineinversetzen*]. Witasek proves that the subject cannot be dealing with a projection, not by analysis of the experience of empathy, but by a logical discussion of possible meanings of projection. It could be a judgment, an assumption, or even a fiction that the empathizing subject is identical with the subject under consideration. Aesthetic empathy does not demonstrate all this and so it is not projection.

Unfortunately, the disjunction is not complete, exactly the possibility applying to the present case being missing. To project oneself into another means to carry out his experience with him as we have described it. Witasek's contention that empathy is an intuitive idea of another's experience only applies to the stage where empathized experiences are made into objects, not to the stage of fulfilling explication. And for this last case we cannot answer the question of whether it is "intuitive in terms of perception or in terms of idea (i.e., non-primordially)" because, as we have shown, empathy is neither one in the usual sense. In fact, it refuses to be classified in one of the current pigeonholes of psychology but will be studied in its own essence.

5. Discussion in Terms of Genetic Theories of the Comprehension of Foreign Consciousness

As we have seen, philosophical investigation has already often come to grips with the problem of foreign consciousness. But its question of how we perceive foreign consciousness has usually <22> taken the turn of how in one psycho-physical individual the perception of another such individual occurs. This has led to the origination of theories of imitation, of inference by analogy, and of empathy by association.

(a) On the Relationship of Phenomenology to Psychology

It may not be superfluous to elucidate the relationship of psychological investigations to what we are doing. Our position is that there is the phenomenon of "foreign experience" and correlatively the "perception of foreign experience." For the present we may leave undecided whether there really is such a foreign experience or whether this perception is authentic. The phenomenon in which all knowledge and certainty must finally be anchored is indubitable. It is the genuine object of πρώτη φιλοσοφία. Thus the first task in this domain, as in all domains, is to comprehend the phenomenon in its pure essence, freed from all the accidents of appearance. What is foreign experience in its givenness? How does the perception of foreign experience look? We must know this before we can ask how this perception occurs.

It is self-evident that this first question cannot in principle be answered by a genetic-psychological investigation of cause,[31] for such an investigation actually presupposes the being whose development it is seeking to ground—its essence as well as the existence, its "what" as well as its "that." Not only the investigation of the nature of the perception of foreign experiencing but also the justification of this perception must thus precede genetic psychology. And if this psychology alleges to accomplish both of these <23> things itself, its claim must be rejected as thoroughly unjustified. This is not to dispute its title to existence in any way. On the contrary, it has its task already very definitely and unequivocally formulated. It is to investigate the origination of the knowledge that a real psycho-physical individual has of other such individuals.

Thus a rigorous delineation of what phenomenology and psychology are to accomplish for the problem of empathy by no means proclaims their complete independence from one another. Indeed, examination of the phenomenological method has shown us that it does not presuppose science in general and especially not a factual science. Thus phenomenology is not tied to the results of genetic psychology, either. On the other hand, psychology pretends to no assertions about the circumstances of the process it is investigating, and it does not occur to phenomenology to encroach upon its privileges. Nevertheless, psychology is entirely bound to the results of phenomenology. Phenomenology investigates the essence of empathy, and wherever empathy is realized this general essence must be retained. Genetic psychology, presupposing the phenomenon of empathy, investigates the process of this realization and must be led back to the phenomenon when its task is completed. If, at the end of the process of origination it delineates, a genetic theory finds something other than that whose origin it wanted to discover, it is condemned. Thus in the results of phenomenological investigation we find a criterion for the utility of genetic theories.

(b) The Theory of Imitation

Now we want to test present genetic theories in terms of our conclusions. Lipps endeavors to explain the experience of foreign psychic life by the doctrine of imitation already familiar to us. (To be sure, it appears in his writings as an element of description.) A witnessed gesture arouses in me the impulse to imitate it. I do this at least "inwardly," if not expressly. Moreover, I have the impulse to express all my experiences. Experience and expression are so closely associated that when one occurs it pulls the other after it. Thus we participate in the experience of the gesture together with this gesture. But, since the experience is experienced "in" the foreign gesture, it does not seem to me to be mine, but another's.

We do not want to go into the objections that can be raised against this theory nor those which have already been raised, with

<24>

or without justification.[32] We only want to employ for criticism what we have already worked out for ourselves. We must therefore say that this theory only distinguishes our own from foreign experience through affiliation with different bodies, while both experiences are actually different in themselves. By the means indicated, I do not arrive at the phenomenon of foreign experience, but at an experience of my own that arouses in me the foreign gestures witnessed. This discrepancy between the phenomenon to be explained and that actually explained suffices as a refutation of this "explanation."

In order to clarify this discrepancy, let us analyze a case of the second kind. We are familiar with the fact that feelings are aroused in us by witnessed "phenomena of expression." A child seeing another crying cries, too. When I see a member of my family going around with a long face, I too become upset. When I want to stop worrying, I seek out happy company. We speak of the contagion or transference of feeling in such cases. It is very plain that the actual feelings aroused in us do not serve a cognitive function, that they do not announce a foreign experience to us as empathy does. So we need not consider whether such a transference of feeling presupposes the comprehension of the foreign feeling concerned, since only phenomena of expression affect us like this. On the contrary, the same change of face interpreted as a grimace certainly can arouse imitation in us, but not a feeling. It is certain that as we are saturated by such "transferred" feelings, we live in them and thus in ourselves. This prevents our turning toward or submerging ourselves in the foreign experience, which is the attitude characteristic of empathy.[33]

<25>

If we had not first comprehended the foreign experience in some other way, we could not have brought it to givenness to ourselves at all. At most we could have concluded the presence of the foreign experience from a feeling in ourselves which required the foreign experience to explain its lack of motivation. But thus we would only have gotten a knowledge of, not a "givenness" of, the foreign experience, as in empathy. It is also possible for this transference itself to be experienced so that I feel the feeling, which was at first a foreign feeling, overflowing me. (For instance, this would be the case if I seek out cheerful company to cheer me up.) Here, too, the difference between comprehending and taking on a feeling is clearly apparent.

Finally, in all cases there is a distinction between the transference of feeling and not only empathy, but also sympathy and a feeling of oneness, these latter being based on an empathic submersion in the foreign experience.[34] From what we have said, it should be sufficiently clear that the theory of imitation cannot serve as a genetic explanation of empathy.

(c) The Theory of Association

The theory of association is a rival of the theory of imitation. The optical image of foreign gestures reproduces the optical image of our own gestures. This reproduces the kinesthesis and this, in turn, the feeling with which the kinesthesis was linked earlier. This feeling is now experienced not as our own, but as foreign, because (1) it faces us as an object, (2) it is not motivated by our own previous experiences, and (3) it is not expressed by a gesture.

<26>

Here, again, we want to raise the question of whether the phenomenon of empathy stands at the end of this process of development. And again the answer is no. By the proposed course we arrive at a feeling of our own and we have grounds for viewing it not as one of our own feelings, but as a foreign one. (At this point we can waive the refutation of these claims.) Now, on these grounds we could conclude that this is another's experience. But in empathy we draw no conclusions because the experience is given as foreign in the character of perception.

Let us illustrate this opposition in a typical case of comprehending foreign psychic life in terms of the theory of association. I see someone stamp his feet. I remember how I myself once stamped my feet at the same time as my previous fury is presented to me. Then I say to myself, "This is how furious he is now." Here the other's fury itself is not given but its existence is inferred. By an intuitive representation, my own fury, I seek to draw it near.[35] By contrast, empathy posits being immediately as a perceived act, and it reaches its object directly without representation. Thus the theory of association also fails to reveal the genesis of empathy.

I realize that this type of associative explanation (Prandtl's) probably does not include all associational psychologists. According to Paul Stern, for example, association is not merely the <27> linking of single ideas, one reproducing another, but is the unity of a perceptual context [*Erfahrungszusammenhang*] in which this context is always before us as a whole. Such a perceptual context is both outside of and within an individual.

But this raises more questions. Certainly association should mean more than the descriptive unity of a perceptual context. It should certainly explain how it arrives at this unity. Thus perhaps all that is given to consciousness at the same time is linked to a whole reproduced as such. But then what distinguishes the unity of the objects of my visual field (that can again arise before me as a whole), from the unity of one object? We cannot do everything in this case with the one word "association." Further, for such a perceptual context to originate, certainly at some time its parts must be given together. But when do I have a person's inner and outer sides given together?

Actually, such cases do occur. Someone has an expression at first unintelligible to me, for instance, he may put his hand over his eyes. On inquiry, I learn that he is meditating deeply on something just now. Now this meditation that I empathize becomes "connected by association" with the perceived pose. When I see this pose again, I see it as a "meditative" pose. Then in this repeated case empathy is, as a matter of fact, based on association. But this association itself requires an empathic act, thus does not suffice as a principle to explain empathy.[36] Furthermore, association only mediates knowledge, for we say to ourselves that this is how he looks when he is meditating. Association does not mediate our understanding of this pose as the expression of an inner condition. This I gain in empathic projection as follows: He is <28> meditating; he has his mind on a problem and wants to shield his train of thought from disturbing distractions; therefore he is covering his eyes and cutting himself off from the outer world.[37]

We must distinguish Volkelt's theory of fusion from this theory of association. Volkelt says that the felt content is not linked with intuition but fused with it. Of course, this is not a genetic explanation but only a description of the empathic experience. Later we

shall return to this phenomenon and see that this viewpoint clari-
fies the origin of certain empathic experiences.[38] This clarification is certainly far from the kind of "exact explanation" the
theory of association is intended to give. Whether such an explanation can be given at all is still in question. This question can
only be decided when the old, much discussed and still so disputed
concept of association has been adequately clarified. Thus we
support Volkelt in his position against Siebeck in which the former maintains that the unity of a material content with its psychic
content is not explained by mere association.[39] On the other
hand, we must agree with Siebeck if he finds a satisfactory genetic
explanation of empathy lacking in Volkelt.[40]

(d) The Theory of Inference by Analogy

The theory of inference by analogy to explain the origin of the
experience of foreign psychic life was almost generally acknowl-
edged before Lipps opposed it. The standpoint of this theory (for
example, J. S. Mill's view) is as follows. There is evidence of outer
and of inner perception, and we can only get at the facts that
<29> these perceptions furnish by means of inferences. This applies to
the present case as follows: I know the foreign physical body and
its modifications; I know my own physical body and its modifications. Further, I know that the modifications of the latter are
conditions and implications of my experiences, likewise given.
Now, because in this case the succession of physical appearances
can only take place when linked with experience, I assume such a
linkage where physical appearances are given alone.

Here, again, we shall only put our old question. Before, we
could point out that the other theories did not lead to the perception of foreign consciousness. Here we see the still more striking
fact that this phenomenon is simply ignored. This theory maintains that we see nothing around us but physical soulless and
lifeless bodies, though I do not see how its advocates could actually hold such a belief.

After our earlier expositions, nothing further is required to
refute the doctrine of inference by analogy as a genetic theory.[41]
Nevertheless, I would like to linger here a little longer in order to
take this odium of complete absurdity from the theory when we

only consider it from the one side. Even so, we cannot deny that inferences by analogy do occur in knowledge of foreign experience. It is easily possible for another's expression to remind me of one of my own so that I ascribe to his expression its usual meaning for me. Only then can we assume the comprehension of another "I" with a bodily expression as a psychic expression. The inference by analogy replaces the empathy perhaps denied. It does not yield perception but a more or less probable knowledge of the foreign experience.[42] Further, this theory does not really intend to give a genetic explanation, though it also occurs as such, and so we must present it here with the others. Rather, it intends to demonstrate the validity of our knowledge of foreign consciousness. It specifies the form in which knowledge of foreign consciousness is "possible." But the value of such an empty form, not oriented toward the nature of knowledge itself, is more than doubtful. Exactly how appropriate the inference by analogy would be for such a demonstration cannot be treated here.   <30>

Thus we conclude from our critical excursions that none of the current genetic theories can account for empathy. Of course, we can guess why this is so. Before one can delineate the genesis of something, one must know what it is.

6. Discussion in Terms of Scheler's Theory of the Comprehension of Foreign Consciousness

We have still to measure empathy against one more theory of foreign consciousness that deviates considerably from all those discussed so far. According to Scheler,[43] we perceive the foreign "I" with its experience inwardly just as we perceive our own "I." (We need not go into his polemic against empathy, since it is not directed against what we call empathy.) Initially there is "a neutral stream of experience" and our "own" and "foreign" experiences are first gradually crystallized out of it. To illustrate this, he cites the fact that we can experience a thought as our own, as foreign, or even as neither of these. Further, initially we do not come upon ourselves as isolated, but as placed in a world of psychic experience. At first we experience our own experiences much less than those of our environment. Finally, out of our own experiences we only perceive what moves along prescribed courses, especially those objects for which we already have a previous term.[44]

<31> This bold theory, standing in opposition to all theories up to now, has something extremely seductive about it. Nevertheless, to get some clarity, we must examine precisely all the concepts used here. Thus we first ask what inner perception is. Scheler answers that inner perception is not the perception of self, for we can perceive ourselves as our bodies outwardly, too. Rather, inner perception is distinguished from outer perception by being directed toward acts. It is the type of act giving us the psychic. These two modes of perception are not to be distinguished on the basis of a difference of objects. Conversely, the physical is to be distinguished from the psychic because, in principle, it is differently given.[45] Nevertheless, Scheler's critique does not seem to corroborate earlier attempts to reciprocally limit psychic and physical[46] by distinguishing criteria. It deals solely with an essential difference of givenness and not with the distinction between objects having different modes of being. To such objects a different mode of givenness would essentially [*wesensgezetslich*] correspond. We could accept "inner perception" in this sense of a definitely constituted act without creating a conflict with our doctrine of empathy. (A more precise explication follows immediately.) It is possible to differentiate within this species of "inner perception" acts in which our own and foreign experience are given.

But this is still not sufficiently clear. What do "own" and "foreign" mean in the context in which Scheler uses them? If we take his discussion of a neutral stream of experience seriously, we cannot conceive of how a differentiation in this stream can occur. But such a stream of experience is an absolutely impossible notion because every experience is by nature an "I's" experience that cannot be separated phenomenally from the "I" itself. It is only because Scheler fails to recognize a pure "I," always taking "I" as

<32> "psychic individual," that he speaks of an experience present before "I's" are constituted. Naturally, he cannot exhibit such an "I-less" experience. Every case he brings up presupposes our own as well as the foreign "I" and does not verify his theory at all.

Only if we leave the phenomenological sphere do these terms make good sense. "Own" and "foreign" then mean: belonging to different individuals, i.e., different substantial, qualitatively elaborated, psychic subjects. Both these individuals and their experiences would be similarly accessible to inner perception. Suppose that I do not feel mine, but foreign feelings. Accordingly, this means that feelings have penetrated my individual from the foreign individual. I am initially surrounded by a world of psychic occurrences, that is to say, at the same time as I discover that my body is in the world of my outer experience against the background of the spatial world spread out boundlessly on all sides, I also discover that my psychic individual is in the world of inner experience, a boundless world of psychic individuals and psychic life.

All this is certainly incontestable. But the basis here is altogether different from ours. We have excluded from the field of our investigation this whole world of inner perception, our own individual and all others, together with the outer world. They are not within, but transcend, the sphere of absolute givenness, of pure consciousness. The "I" has another meaning in this sphere of absolute consciousness, being nothing but the subject of experience living in experience. In these terms, the question of whether an experience is "mine" or another's becomes senseless. What I primordially feel is precisely what I feel irrespective of this feeling's role in the sum total of my individual experiences or of how it originates (perhaps by contagion of feeling or not).[47] These experiences of my own, the pure experiences of the pure "I," are given to me in reflection. This means that the "I" turns back and away from its object and looks at the experience of this object.

Now what distinguishes reflection from inner perception, more   <33> exactly, from the inner perception of self? Reflection is always an actual turning toward an actual experience, while inner perception itself can be non-actual. In principle, it can also encompass the fringe of non-actualities that form my present experience together with perception. Further, I may view my experiences in such a way that I no longer consider them as such, but as evidence of the transcendence of my individual and its attributes. My recollections announce my memory to me; my acts of outer perception announce the acuteness of my senses (not to be taken as sense organs, of course); my volition and conduct announce my energy, etc. And these attributes declare the nature of my individual to me. We can designate this viewing as inner perception of self.

We have reliable evidence for the contention that Scheler's "inner perception" is the apperception of "self" in the sense of the individual and his experiences within the context of individual experience. He ascribes complexes of experience to the objects of inner perception which come to givenness in a uniform intuitive act, for example, my childhood.[48] (Of course, I would not call this perception, but one of those "abridgments of memory" [*Erinnerungsabrêgés*] alluded to earlier. We must reserve an analysis of this for the phenomenology of representational consciousness.)

Further, he means that the "totality of our 'I'" is given in inner perception just as in the act of outer perception; not single sensual qualities, but the totality of nature is given.[49] Scheler could not characterize this totality more clearly than as an apperception of a transcendence even if he stressed the difference between the unity in variety characteristic of inner and of outer perception (or "separateness" and "togetherness").[50] This "I" is fundamentally different from the pure "I," the subject of actual experience. The unities constituted in inner perception are different from the unity of having an experience. And the inner perception giving us these complexes of experience is different from the reflection in which we comprehend the absolute being of an actual experience.

<34> Scheler himself distinguishes between reflection and inner perception,[51] which he denies is a comprehension of acts in contrast with reflection. Thus it is still more striking that he did not see the distinction between his own and Husserl's concept of "inner perception," and that he even carries on a polemic against Husserl's preference for inner perception over outer.[52] Precisely because the term "inner perception" could have a number of meanings, Husserl substituted "reflection" for it to designate the absolute givenness of experience.[53] Nor would he say that inner perception in Scheler's sense was more conclusive than outer perception.

The difference between reflection and inner perception also becomes very clear in a consideration of the deceptions of inner perception presented in Scheler's *Idolenlehre*. Should I be deceived in my feelings for another person, this deception cannot mean that I comprehend an act of love by reflection that is not present in fact. There is no such "reflective deception." Should I comprehend an actual erotic emotion in reflection, I have an absolute not to be interpreted away in any manner. I can be deceived in the object of my love, i.e., the person I thought I comprehended in this act may in fact be different, so that I comprehended a phantom. But the love was still genuine. Perhaps, also, the love does not endure as one expected, but ceases very shortly. This is not a reason, either, for saying it was not genuine as long as it lasted. But Scheler is not thinking of such deceptions.

The first kind of "idol" he presents is a deceptive directing. As we live in the feelings of our environment, we take them for our own, though they do not clarify our own feelings at all. We take <35> feelings "acquired by reading" to be our own. For instance, the young girl thinks she feels Juliet's love.[54]

I think we still need distinctions and thorough analyses here. Suppose that I have taken over from my environment a hatred and contempt for the members of a particular race or party. For example, as the child of conservative parents, I may hate Jews and social democrats, or raised with more liberal views, I may hate "Junkers" [aristocratic landowners]. Then this would be an entirely genuine and sincere hatred save for the fact that it is based on an empathic valuing, rather than on a primordial one. This hatred may also be increased by contagion of feeling to such a degree that it is not legitimately related to the felt disvalue. Thus I am not under a deception when I comprehend my hatred. Two deceptions can be present here: (1) a deception of value (as I think I comprehend a disvalue that does not exist at all); (2) a deception about my person, if I were to imagine, on the basis of my own insight, that these feelings are exalted and view my prejudice as "loyalty." In the second case there is really a deception of inner perception but certainly not a deception of reflection.[55] I cannot be clear in reflection about the failure of the basic primordial valuing because I cannot reflect on an act that is not present. But should I carry out such an act and bring it to givenness to myself, I gain clarity and thus also the possibility of unmasking the earlier deception by comparing it with this case.

Feelings "acquired by reading" are no different. Should the enamored schoolboy think he feels Romeo's passion, this does not mean he believes he has a stronger feeling than is actually present. He actually feels passion because he has blown his spark into a flame by borrowed embers. This flame will go out of its own accord as soon as the embers die out. Because a

<36> primordial valuing is lacking as a foundation, we also have "non-genuineness" here. This results in a false relationship between the feeling, on the one hand, and its subject and object, on the other. And the youth's deception is that he attributes Romeo's passion to himself, not that he thinks he has a strong feeling.

Now let us look at the other deceptive directing where experiences actually present do not come to givenness. I do not see how we can call a feeling actually present a deception if, because it is beyond traditional lines, it is not perceived. The turning toward our own experience naturally means the cessation of the foreign attitude. It requires special circumstances to direct attention to our own experiencing. Thus, if I do not notice a feeling because nothing has made me aware that there is "such a thing," this is entirely natural and is deceptive as little as my not hearing a sound in my environment or overlooking an object in my visual field.[56] Scheler is certainly not discussing deceptive reflection, for "reflection" is the comprehension of an experience, and it is trivial to say that an experience I comprehend does not elude me. It is a different story if the experience does not elude me but I take it, rather, to be imagined because it does not fit in with my environment. Here it seems that I do not want to participate in this experience and would like to get it entirely out of my world. It is not that I think the experience is non-primordial and am actually deceived.

If the motive of our behavior deceives us,[57] we are, again, not

<37> perceiving a motive in reflection that is not present. Either we experience no clearly conscious motive for our conduct or there

are other motives operating besides the motive before us. We cannot bring these other motives clearly to givenness to ourselves because they are not actual, but "background," experiences. For the reflecting glance to be directed toward an experience, this experience must assume the form of a specific "cogito." For example, suppose that I go into the military service as a·volunteer under the impression that I am doing so out of pure patriotism and do not notice that a longing for adventure, vanity, or a dissatisfaction with my present situation also play a part. Then these secondary motives withdraw from my reflecting glance just as if they were not yet, or no longer, actual. I am thus under an inner perceptual and value deception if I take this action as it appears to me and interpret it as evidence of a noble character. People are generally inclined to ascribe to themselves better motives than they actually have and are not conscious of many of their emotional impulses at all[58] because these feelings already seem to have a disvalue in the mode of non-actuality, and people do not allow them to become actual at all. But this does not cause the feelings to cease enduring or functioning. The fact that we can feel past or future events to be valuable or worthless when they themselves are no longer, or not yet, "conceived" is also based on this difference between actuality and non-actuality.[59] Thus, an actual valuing can be based on a non-actual memory or expectation. We can hardly hold that this would be a pure valuing without a basic, theoretical act. There are no such experiences contradicting the essence of the experience of value.

Scheler is also dealing with "background experiences" when he says that the same experience can be perceived more or less exactly.[60] A pain that "entirely disappears from our glance or is only present as a very general impression while we are laughing and joking" is a non-actual experience persisting in the background while the "I" is living in other actualities. We can only say <38> that an experience is differently "presented" in the contexts of the perceptions into which it enters. No matter how figuratively we take it, an experience comprehended in reflection has no "sides."

In conclusion, by this contrast we can understand why Scheler distinguishes between "peripheral" experiences that sever one

another in sequence and "central" experiences that are given as a
unity revealing the unity of the "I." We have a sequence at all
levels in the sense that one actual experience severs another. But
some experiences disappear as soon as they have faded out (a
sensory pain, a sensory delight, an act of perception), while others
continue to endure in the mode of non-actuality. The latter form
those unities that enable us to glance perceptually back into the
past (at a love, a hatred, a friendship), and they constitute the
complex structure that can come to givenness to us in an intuitive
act, such as my childhood, my student days, etc.[61] I hope this
exhibits the difference between reflection in which actual experience is given to us absolutely and inner perception in general.
Also this should indicate the difference between the complex
unities based on these different acts and the individual "I" revealing itself in them.[62]

Now we can already see the relationship between inner perception and empathy. Just as our own individual is announced in our
own perceived experiences, so the foreign individual is announced in empathized ones. But we also see that in one case
there is a primordial, while in the other a non-primordial,
givenness of the constituting experiences. If I experience a feeling as that of another, I have it given twice: once primordially as
my own and once non-primordially in empathy as originally foreign. And precisely this non-primordiality of empathized experiences causes me to reject the general term "inner perception" for
<39> the comprehension of our own and foreign experience.[63] Should
one desire to stress what these two experiences have in common,
it would be better to say "inner intuition" [*innere Anschauung*].
This would include, then, the non-primordial givenness of our
own experiences in memory, expectation, or fantasy.

But there is still another reason why I object to including empathy under inner perception. There is really only a parallel on the
level of empathy where I have the foreign experience facing me.
The level where I am at the foreign "I" and explain its experience by living it after the other seems to be much more parallel to
the primordial experience itself than to its givenness in inner
perception.

7. Münsterberg's Theory of the Experience of Foreign Consciousness

It is still more difficult for me to sift the phenomenal content out of Münsterberg's theory than it was in Scheler. Our experience of foreign subjects is to consist of the understanding of foreign acts of will. He agrees with our analysis by characterizing this act of understanding as an act in which the "foreign will enters into mine" and still remains that of the other. But we cannot see why this understanding should be confined to acts of will. As we saw, it applies to all kinds of empathic acts. Now Münsterberg takes "act of will" in a broader sense. He includes under it all "attitudes" that "anticipate," this anticipating clinging to attitudes for the one who comprehends them.

But we cannot accept his thesis even in this broader sense. An empathized mood is an experience of foreign consciousness in the same sense as an empathized attitude is. Both include comprehending the foreign subject. What distinguishes attitudes is that the anticipation inherent in them contains a contrast between the one and the other subject not found in other cases.

Münsterberg believes he has an immediate awareness of foreign subjects here that precedes the constitution of the individual. To gain access to these lines of thought, we must pursue the constitution of the individual. And this will be our next undertaking. <40>

Chapter III

The Constitution of the
Psycho-Physical Individual

W e have now achieved an essential description of the empathic act and a critique of historical theories of foreign consciousness from the point of view of our description. We still have a far greater undertaking before us. We must treat empathy as a problem of constitution and answer the question of how the objects in the usual theories, such as the psycho-physical individual, personality, etc., arise within consciousness.

Within the framework of a short investigation we cannot hope even to approach the answer to this question. We shall have fulfilled our purpose if we succeed in showing the paths to this goal and that the investigations of empathy so far could not be satisfactory because, except for a very few attempts, these thinkers have overlooked these basic questions. This is very clear in Lipps, who has certainly achieved the most progress toward our goal. He seems to be bound by the phenomenon of the expression of experiences and repeatedly comes back to that from which he also wants to begin. With a few words he lays aside the profusion of questions present in the treatment of this problem. For instance, he says about the bearer of these phenomena of expression, "We believe a conscious life to be bound to certain bodies by virtue of an 'inexplicable adjustment of our spirit' or a 'natural instinct.'"

This is nothing more than the proclamation of wonder, declar-   <41>

37

ing the bankruptcy of scientific investigation. And if science is not permitted to do this, then especially not philosophy. For here there is no longer any domain into which it can push unsolved questions as all other disciplines can. This means that philosophy must give the final answer, gain final clarity. We have final clarity and no questions remain open when we have achieved what we call progress—the constitution of transcendental objects in immanently given, pure consciousness. This is the goal of phenomenology.

Now let us turn to the constitution of the individual and make clear, in the first place, what an individual is.

1. The Pure "I"

So far we have always spoken of the pure "I" as the otherwise indescribable, qualityless subject of experience. In various authors, such as Lipps, we have found the interpretation that this is not an "individual 'I'" but first becomes individual in contrast with "you" and "he." What does this individuality mean? First of all, it means only that it is "itself" and no other. This "selfness" is experienced and is the basis of all that is "mine." Naturally, it is first brought into relief in contrast with another when another is given. This other is at first not qualitatively distinguished from it, since both are qualityless, but only distinguished as simply an "other." This otherness is apparent in the type of givenness; it is other than "I" because it is given to me in another way than "I." Therefore it is "you." But, since it experiences itself as I experience myself, the "you" is another "I." Thus the "I" does not become individualized because another faces it, but its individuality, or as we would rather say (because we must reserve the term "individuality" for something else), its selfness is brought into relief in contrast with the otherness of the other.

2. The Stream of Consciousness

We can take the "I" in a second sense as the unity of a stream of
<42>   consciousness. We begin with the "I" as the subject of an actual experience. However, when we reflect on this experience, we find that it is not isolated, but set against the background of a stream of such experiences more or less clearly and distinctly

given. The "I" of this experience was not always in it but shifted over or was drawn into it from another experience, and so on. Going over these experiences, we continually come upon experiences in which the present "I" had once lived. This is even true when we can no longer directly grasp the experience, finding it necessary to view it through remembering representation.

Precisely this affiliation of all the stream's experiences with the present, living, pure "I" constitutes its inviolable unity. Now "other" streams of consciousness face this "same" stream; the stream of the "I" faces those of the "you" and the "he." Their selfness and otherness are based on those of their subject. However, they are not only "others," but also "varied" because each one has its peculiar experiential content. Since every single experience of a stream is particularly characterized by its position in the total experiential context, it is also characterized apart from belonging to an "I." Thus it is also qualitative as the experience of this and no other "I," and streams of consciousness are qualitatively distinguished by virtue of their experiential content. But even this qualitative distinction does not yet take us to what is usually understood by an individual "I" or an individual.

The stream of consciousness, characterized as "it itself and no other" with a nature peculiar to it, results in a good sense of precisely limited individuality. Qualitative peculiarity without selfness would be insufficient for individualization because we can also arrive at qualitative variation of the stream of consciousness by thinking of the one given stream as qualitatively modified in the course of experience. This does not mean that its affiliation with the same "I" ceases; the stream only becomes another by   <43> belonging to another "I." Selfness and qualitative variation together—thus individuality in two senses—constitute a further step in progress to the "individual 'I'" of common parlance, i.e., a characteristically structured psycho-physical unity.

3. The Soul

Next we can examine the individual unity of the psyche as such while neglecting the living body and psycho-physical relationships. Our uniform, isolated stream of consciousness is not our soul. But, as we already saw in examining inner perception, among our experiences there is one basic experience given to us which, together with its persistent attributes, becomes apparent in our experiences as the identical "bearer" of them. This is the substantial soul. We have already become acquainted with single such psychic attributes, too. The acuteness of our senses apparent in our outer perceptions is such an attribute. Another is the energy apparent in our conduct. The tension or laxity of our volitions manifests the vivacity and strength or the weakness of our will. Its persistence is found in its duration. The intensity of our feelings, the ease with which they appear, the excitability of our sentiments, etc. disclose our disposition.

It is hardly necessary to follow out these relationships further. We take the soul to be a substantial unity which, entirely analogous to the physical thing, is made up of categorical elements and the sequence of categories. Its elements appear as individual instances of these categories, and the soul forms a parallel to the sequence of experiential categories. Among these categorical elements there are some that point beyond the isolated soul to connections with other psychic as well as physical unities, to impressions which the soul makes and suffers. "Causality" and "changeability" are also among the psychic categories.

<44> This substantial unity is "my" soul when the experiences in which it is apparent are "my" experiences or acts in which my pure "I" lives. The peculiar structure of psychic unity depends on the peculiar content of the stream of experience; and, conversely, (as we must say after the soul has been constituted for us) the content of the stream of experience depends on the structure of the soul. Were there streams of consciousness alike in content,[64] there would also be souls of the same kind or instances of ideally-the-same soul. However, we do not have the complete psychic phenomenon (nor the psychic individual) when we examine it in isolation.

4. "I" and Living Body

For greater clarity here, we must now take a step that we have been reluctant to take until the course of the investigation demanded it. This is the step from psychic to psycho-physical. Our proposed division between soul and body was an artificial one, for the soul is always necessarily a soul in a body. What is the body? How and as what is it given to us?

(a) The Givenness of the Living Body

We again proceed from the sphere forming the basis of all our investigations: that of pure consciousness. How is my body [*Leib*] constituted within consciousness? I have my physical body [*Körper*] given once in acts of outer perception. But if we suppose it to be given to us in this manner alone, we have the strangest object. This would be a real thing, a physical body, whose motivated successive appearances exhibit striking gaps. It would withhold its rear side with more stubbornness than the moon and invite me continually to consider it from new sides. Yet as soon as I am about to carry out its invitation, it hides these sides from me. To be sure, things that withdraw from the glance are accessible to touch. But precisely the relationship between seeing and touching is different here than anywhere else. Everything else I see says to me, "Touch me. I am really what I seem to be, am tangible, <45> and not a phantom." And what I touch calls to me, "Open your eyes and you will see me." The tactile and visual senses (as one can speak of sense in the pure sphere) call each other as witnesses, though they do not shift the responsibility on one another.

This unique defect of the outwardly perceived physical body is in contrast with another peculiarity. I can approach and withdraw from any other thing, can turn toward or away from it. In the latter case, it vanishes from my sight. This approaching and withdrawing, the movement of my physical body and of other things, is documented by an alteration of their successive appearances. A distinction between these two cases: the movement of other things and the movement of my physical body, is inconceivable. Nor is it possible to see how we comprehend the movement of our own physical bodies at all as long as we maintain the fiction that our physical body is only constituted in outer perception and not as a characteristically living body. Thus we must say, more precisely, that every other object is given to me in an infinitely variable multiplicity of appearances and of changing positions, and there are also times when it is not given to me. But this one object (my physical body) is given to me in successive appearances only variable within very narrow limits. As long as I have my eyes open at all, it is continually there with a steadfast obtrusiveness, always having the same tangible nearness as no other object has. It is always "here" while other objects are always "there."

But this brings us to the limit of our supposition and we must suspend it. For even if we shut our eyes tightly and stretch out our arms, in fact allowing no limb to contact another so that we can neither touch nor see our physical body, even then we are not rid of it. Even then it stands there inescapably in full embodiment (hence the name), and we find ourselves bound to it perpetually. Precisely this affiliation, this belonging to me, could never be constituted in outer perception. A living body [*Leib*] only perceived outwardly would always be only a particularly disposed, actually unique, physical body, but never "my living body."

<46>

Now let us observe how this new givenness occurs. As an instance of the supreme category of "experience," sensations are among the real constituents of consciousness, of this domain impossible to cancel. The sensation of pressure or pain or cold is just as absolutely given as the experience of judging, willing, perceiving, etc. Yet, in contrast with these acts, sensation is peculiarly characterized. It does not issue from the pure "I" as they do, and it never takes on the form of the "cogito" in which the "I" turns toward an object. Since sensation is always spatially localized "somewhere" at a distance from the "I" (perhaps very near to it but never in it), I can never find the "I" in it by reflection. And this "somewhere" is not an empty point in space, but something filling up space. All these entities from which my sensations arise are amalgamated into a unity, the unity of my living body, and they are themselves places in the living body.

There are differences in this unified givenness in which the living body is always there for me as a whole. The various parts of the living body constituted for me in terms of sensation are various distances from me. Thus my torso is nearer to me than my extremities, and it makes good sense to say that I bring my hands near or move them away. To speak of distance from "me" is inexact because I cannot really establish an interval from the "I," for it is non-spatial and cannot be localized. But I relate the parts of my living body, together with everything spatial outside of it, to a "zero point of orientation" which my living body surrounds. This zero point is not to be geometrically localized at one point in my physical body; nor is it the same for all data. It is localized in the head for visual data and in mid-body for tactile data. Thus, whatever refers to the "I" has no distance from the zero point, and all that is given at a distance from the zero point is also given at a distance from the "I."

However, this distance of bodily parts from me is fundamentally different from the distance of other things from each other and from me. Two things in space are at a specific distance   <47> from each other. They can approach each other and even come into contact, whereupon their distance disappears. It is also possible (if the objects are not materially impenetrable, but, for instance, are hallucinatory objects of different visual hallucinators) for them to occupy the same portion of space. Similarly, a thing can approach me, its distance from me can decrease, and it can contact not me, but my physical body. Then the distance from my physical body, but not from me, becomes zero. Nor does the distance of the thing from the zero point become the same as the distance of the contacted part of the physical body from the zero point. I could never say that the stone I hold in my hand is the same distance or "only a tiny bit farther" from the zero point than the hand itself.

The distance of the parts of my living body from me is completely incomparable with the distance of foreign physical bodies from me. The living body as a whole is at the zero point of orientation with all physical bodies outside of it. "Body space" [*Leibraum*] and "outer space" are completely different from each other. Merely perceiving outwardly, I would not arrive at the living body, nor merely "perceiving bodily" [*Leibwahrnehmend*], at the outer world. But the living body is constituted in a two-fold manner as a sensed (bodily perceived) living body and as an outwardly perceived physical body of the outer world. And in this doubled givenness it is experienced as the same. Therefore, it has a location in outer space and fills up a portion of this space.

There is still something to say about the relationship between sensation and "bodily perception." The analysis of sensations usually comes up in other contexts. We usually look at sensations as what "give" us the outer world, and in this sense we separate "sensation" from "what is sensed" or "content of sensation" from "sensation as function" in Stumpf's sense. We separate, for example, the seen red and the possessing of this red.[65] I cannot agree with him. The object's red is "perceived" and I must distinguish between perception and what is perceived. The analysis of perception leads me to "sensory data" so that I can look at the perception of qualities as an "objectification of sensory data." But this does not make qualities into perceptions nor perceptions into qualities or giving acts. As constituents of outer perception, both are elements not further analyzable.

<48>

Now if we consider sensation in terms of the side turned toward the living body, we find an entirely analogous phenomenal state of affairs. I can speak of a "sensed" living body as little as of a "sensed" object in the outer world. However, this also requires an objectifying apprehension. If my fingertips contact the table, I have to distinguish, first, the sensation of touch, the tactile datum not further divisible. Secondly, there is the hardness of the table with its correlative act of outer perception and, thirdly, the touching fingertip and the correlative act of "bodily perception." What makes the connection between sensation and bodily perception particularly intimate is the fact that sensations are given at the living body to the living body as senser.

An investigation of all kinds of sensations in their meaning for bodily perception would be beyond the scope of this work. But we must discuss one more point. We said that the "outer" and "bodily perceived" living body is given as the same. This requires still further elucidation. I not only see my hand and bodily perceive it as sensing, but I also "see" its fields of sensation constituted for me in bodily perception. On the other hand, if I consciously emphasize certain parts of my living body, I have an "image" of this part of the physical body. The one is given with the other, though they are not perceived together. This is exactly analogous to the province of outer perception. We not only see the table and feel its hardness, but we also "see" its hardness. The robes in Van Dyck's paintings are not only as shiny as silk but also as smooth and as soft as silk. Psychologists call this phenomenon fusion and usually reduce it to "mere association." This "mere" indicates psychology's tendency to look at explanation as an explaining away, so that the explained phenomenon becomes a <49> "subjective creation" without "objective meaning." We cannot accept this interpretation. Phenomenon remains phenomenon. An explanation is very desirable, but this explanation adds nothing to or subtracts nothing from it. Thus the certainty of tactile qualities would continue to exist and lose none of its merit whether or not association can explain it.

To be sure, we do not think such an explanation possible because it contradicts the "phenomenon" of association. Association is typically experienced as "something reminding me of something." For example, the sight of the table corner reminds me I once bumped myself on it. However, this corner's sharpness is not remembered, but seen. Here is another instructive example: I see a rough lump of sugar and know or remember that it is sweet. I do not remember it is rough (or only incidentally), nor see its sweetness. By contrast, the flower's fragrance is really sweet and does not remind me of a sweet taste. This begins to open up perspectives for a phenomenology of the senses and of sense perceptions that, of course, we cannot go into here. At this point we are only interested in applying these insights to our case. The seen living body does not remind us it can be the scene of manifold sensations. Neither is it merely a physical thing taking up the same space as the living body given as sensitive in bodily perception. It is given as a sensing, living body.

So far we have only considered the living body at rest. Now we can go a step farther. Let us suppose that I (i.e., my living body as a whole) move through the room. As long as we disregarded the constitution of the living body, this was not a peculiarly characterized phenomenon. It was no different than the kaleidoscopic shifting of the surrounding outer world. Now the experience that "I move" becomes entirely new. It becomes the apperception of our own movement based on manifold sensations and is entirely different from the outwardly perceived movement of physical bodies. Now the comprehension of our own movement and the alteration of the outer world are combined in the form of "if <50> . . . then." "If I move, then the picture of my environment shifts."

This is just as true for the perception of the single spatial thing as for the cohesive spatial world, and, similarly, for movements of parts of the living body as for its movement as a whole. If I rest my hand on a rotating ball, this ball and its movement are given to me as a succession of changing tactile data merging into an intention permeating the whole. These data can be comprehended together in an "apperceptive grasp," a unified act of outer perception. Data have the same sequence if my hand glides over the still ball, but the experience that "I move" supervenes anew and, with the apperception of the ball, goes into the form of "if . . . then." Visual data are analogous. While being still, I can see the changing appearances of a rolling ball; and the "shades of the ball" can look the same if the ball is still and I move my head or only my eyes. This movement, again, is given to me in "bodily perception."

This is how parts of the living body are constituted as moving organs and the perception of the spatial world as dependent on the behavior of these organs. But this does not yet show us how we comprehend the movements of living bodies as movements of physical bodies. When I move one of my limbs, besides becoming bodily aware of my own movement, I have an outer visual or tactile perception of physical body movements to which the limb's changed appearances testify. As the bodily perceived and outwardly perceived limb are interpreted as the same, so there also arises an identical coincidence of the living and physical body's movement. The moving living body becomes the moved physical body. And the fact that "I move" is "seen with" the movement of a part of my physical body. The unseen movement of the physical body in the experience of "I move" is comprehended jointly.

The affiliation of the "I" with the perceiving body requires some further elucidation. The impossibility of being rid of the body indicates its special givenness. This union cannot be shaken; the bonds tying us to our bodies are indissoluble. Nevertheless, we are permitted certain liberties. All the objects in the outer world have a certain distance from me. They are always "there" while I am always here. They are grouped around me, around my "here." This grouping is not rigid and unchangeable. Objects approach and withdraw from me and from one another, and I

<51>

myself can undertake a regrouping by moving things farther or nearer or exchanging their places. Or else I can take another "standpoint" so that I change my "here" instead of their "there." Every step I take discloses a new bit of the world to me or I see the old one from a new side. In so doing I always take my living body along. Not only I am always "here" but also it is; the various "distances" of its parts from me are only variations within this "here."

Now, instead of in reality, I can also "regroup" my environment "in thought alone." I can fantasize. For example, I can fantasize my room empty of furniture and "imagine" how it would look then. I can also take an excursion through the world of fantasy. "In thought" I can get up from my desk, go into a corner of the room, and regard it from there. Here I do not take my living body along. Perhaps the "I" standing there in the corner has a fantasized living body, i.e., one seen in "bodily fantasy," if I may say so. Moreover, this body can look at the living body [*Leibkörper*] at the desk it has left just as well as at other things in the room. Of course, this living body then also is a represented object, i.e., one given in representing outer intuition. Finally, the real living body [*Leib*] has not disappeared, but I actually continue to sit at my desk unsevered from my living body. Thus my "I" has been doubled,[66] and, even though the real "I" cannot be released from its body, there is at least the possibility of "slipping out of one's skin" in fantasy. <52>

An "I" without a body is a possibility.[67] But a body without an "I" is utterly impossible. To fantasize my body forsaken by my "I" means to fantasize my living body no longer, but a completely parallel physical body, to fantasize my corpse. (If I leave my living body, it becomes for me a physical body like others. And, instead of my leaving it, should I think of it away from me, this removal is not "one's own movement" but a pure movement of the physical body. There is still another way of showing this. A "withered" limb without sensations is not part of my living body. A foot "gone to sleep" is an appendage like a foreign physical body that I cannot shake off. It lies beyond the spatial zone of my living body into which it is once more drawn when it "awakens." Every movement I make of it in this condition is like "moving an object," i.e.,

my alive movement evokes a mechanical movement. And this
moving itself is not given as the living moving of a living body. For
<53> the living body is essentially constituted through sensations; sen-
sations are real constituents of consciousness and, as such, belong
to the "I." Thus how could there be a living body not the body of
an "I"?[68]

Whether a sensing "I" is conceivable without a living body is
another question. This is the question of whether there could be
sensations in which no living body is constituted. The answer can
be given without further ado because, as already stated, the sensations of the various sensory provinces do not share in the structure of the living body in the same manner. Thus we have to assay
whether the localization of the senses clearly experienced at
places in the living body—of taste, temperature, or pain—is necessary and incommutable. If this is the case, it would make them
possible only for a living bodily "I" so that another analysis of the
senses of sight, hearing, etc. would still seem to be necessary.

We need not decide these questions here, though a phenomenology of outer perception would not be able to avoid them. Nevertheless, the senses have already constituted the unity of "I" and
living body for us, even though not the complete range of reciprocal relationships as yet. Also the causal relationship between
the psychic and the physical already confronts us in the province
of the senses. Purely physical events such as a foreign body being
forced under my skin or a certain amount of heat coming into
contact with the surface of my physical body is the phenomenal
cause [*Ursache*] of sensations of pain and of temperature. It turns
out to be "stimulation." We shall come upon such phenomenal
causal relationships often now as we further pursue the relationships between soul and living body.

(b) The Living Body and Feelings

Sensations of feelings [*Gefühlsempfindungen*] or sensual feelings
[*sinnlichen Gefühle*] are inseparable from their founding sensations. The pleasantness of a savory dish, the agony of a sensual
pain, the comfort of a soft garment are noticed where the food is
tasted, where the pain pierces, where the garment clings to the
body's surface. However, sensual feelings not only are there but

at the same time also in me; they issue from my "I." General feelings have a hybrid position similar to sensual feelings. Not only the "I" feels vigorous or sluggish, but I "notice this in all my limbs." Every mental act, every joy, every pain, every activity of thought, together with every bodily action, every movement I make, is sluggish and colorless when "I" feel sluggish. My living body and all its parts are sluggish with me. Thus our familiar <54> phenomenon of fusion again appears. Not only do I see my hand's movement and feel its sluggishness at the same time, but I also see the sluggish movement and the hand's sluggishness. We always experience general feelings as coming from the living body with an accelerating or hindering influence on the course of experience. This is true even when these general feelings arise in connection with a "spiritual feeling."

Moods are "general feelings" of a non-somatic nature, and so we separate them from strictly general feeling as a species of their own. Cheerfulness and melancholy do not fill the living body. It is not cheerful or melancholy as it is vigorous or sluggish, nor could a purely spiritual being be subject to moods. But this does not imply that psychic and bodily general feelings run beside one another undisturbed. Rather, one seems to have a reciprocal "influence" on the other. For instance, suppose I take a trip to recuperate and arrive at a sunny, pleasant spot. While looking at the view, I feel that a cheerful mood wants to take possession of me, but cannot prevail because I feel sluggish and tired. "I shall be cheerful here as soon as I have rested up," I say to myself. I may know this from "previous experience," yet its foundation is always in the phenomenon of the reciprocal action of psychic and somatic experiences.

(c) Soul and Living Body, Psycho-Physical Causality

The psychic is in essence characterized by this dependence of experiences on somatic influences. Everything psychic is body-bound consciousness, and in this area essentially psychic experiences, body-bound sensations, etc., are distinguished from accidental physical experiences, the "realizations" of spiritual life.[69] As the substantial unity announced in single psychic experiences, the soul is based on the living body. This is shown in the phenomenon of "psycho-physical causality" we have delineated and in the nature of sensations. And the soul together with the living body forms the "psycho-physical" individual.

<55>   Now we must consider the character of so-called "spiritual feelings." The term already indicates to us that spiritual feelings are accidentally psychic and not body-bound (even if psychologists would not like to acknowledge this consequence.) Anyone who brings the pure essence of a bodiless subject to givenness would contend that such a subject experiences no pleasure, grief, or aesthetic values. By contrast, many noted psychologists see "complexes of organic sensations" in feelings. As absurd as this definition may seem as long as we consider feelings in their pure essence, in concrete psychic contexts we actually do find phenomena which do not ground feelings, to be sure, though they can make them intelligible. "Our heart stops beating" for joy; we "wince" in pain; our pulse races in alarm; and we are breathless. Examples which all deal with psycho-physical causality, with effects of psychic experience on body functions, can be multiplied at will. When we think the living body away, these phenomena disappear, though the spiritual act remains. It must be conceded that God rejoices over the repentance of a sinner without feeling His heart pound or other "organic sensations," an observation that is possible whether one believes in God or not. People can be convinced that in reality feelings are impossible without such sensations and that no existing being experiences them in their purity. However, feelings can be comprehended in their purity. and this appearance of accompaniment is experienced exactly as such, as neither a feeling nor a component of one. The same thing can also be shown in cases of purely psychic causality. "I lose my wits" for fright, i.e., I notice my thoughts are paralyzed. Or "my head spins" for joy so that I do not know what I am doing and do pointless things. A pure spirit can also become frightened but it does not lose its wits. [Its understanding does not stand still.] It feels pleasure and pain in all their depth without these feelings exerting any effect.

              I can expand these considerations. As I "observe" myself, I also
<56>   discover causal relationships between my experiences with their announced capacities and the attributes of my soul. Capacities can

be developed and sharpened by use as well as worn out and dulled. Thus my "power of observation" increases as I work in natural science; for example, my power for distinguishing colors as I work with sorting threads of finely shaded colors, my "capacity for enjoyment" as I have pleasures. Every capacity can be strengthened by "training." On the other hand, at a certain "habituation" point the opposite effect takes place. I "get enough of" an "object of pleasure" continually placed before me. It eventually arouses boredom, disgust, etc. In all these cases the physical is phenomenally having an effect on the psychic. But it is a question of what kind of an "effect" this is and of whether this phenomenon of causality enables us to arrive at an exact concept of causality for natural science and at a general law of cause. Exact natural science is based on this concept, while descriptive science deals only with the phenomenal concept of causality. It is also the case that an exact concept of causality and unbroken causal precision are a presupposition of the exact causal-genetic psychology to which psychologists aspire in conjunction with the example set by the modern science of physical nature. We must content ourselves here with pointing out these problems without going into their solution.[70]

(d) The Phenomenon of Expression

The consideration of the causal operation of feelings has led us further than we anticipated. Nevertheless, we have not exhausted what feelings can teach us. There arises a new phenomenon of the expression of feeling beside this appearance of accompaniment. I blush for shame, I irately clench my fist, I angrily furrow my brow, I groan with pain, am jubilant with joy. The relationship of feeling to expression is completely different from that of feeling to the appearance of physical accompaniment. In the former case I do not notice physical experiences issuing out of psychic ones, much less their mere simultaneity. Rather, as I live through the feeling, I feel it terminate in an expression or release expression out of itself.[71] Feeling in its pure essence is not something complete in itself. As it were, it is loaded with an energy which must be unloaded.

This unloading is possible in different ways. We know one kind

<57>

of unloading very well. Feelings release or motivate volitions and actions, so to speak. Feeling is related to the appearance of expression in exactly the same way. The same feeling that motivates a volition can also motivate an appearance of expression. And feeling by its nature prescribes what expression and what volition it can motivate.[72] By nature it must always motivate something, must always be "expressed." Only different forms of expression are possible.

<58>   It could be objected here that in life feelings often arise without motivating a volition or bodily expression. As is well-known, we civilized people must "control" ourselves and hold back the bodily expression of our feelings. We are similarly restricted in our activities and thus in our volitions. There is, of course, still the loophole of "airing" one's wishes. The employee who is allowed neither to tell his superior by contemptuous looks he thinks him a scoundrel or a fool nor to decide to remove him, can still wish secretly that he would go to the devil. Or one can carry out deeds in fantasy that are blocked in reality. One who is born into restricted circumstances and cannot fulfill himself in reality carries out his desire for great things by winning battles and performing wonders of valor in imagination. The creation of another world where I can do what is forbidden to me here is itself a form of expression. Thus the man dying of thirst sees in the distance before him oases with bubbling springs or seas that revive him, as Gebsattel reports.[73]

The joy filling us is not a meditative devotion to the pleasing object. Rather, it is externalized in other situations as we entirely surround ourselves with what is enjoyable. We seek it in our real surrounding world or induce it by memory or freely fantasizing representation. We neglect everything that does not fit in with it until our frame of mind is in complete harmony with our surrounding world.

This peculiarity of expression requires a comprehensive clarification. It is not enough to state that feelings influence the "reproduction of ideas" and how frequently this occurs, as psychology usually does.

But expression or its surrogate is possible in still another way, and to this the "controlled" person who for social, aesthetic, or ethical reasons puts on a uniform countenance in public usually retreats. Feeling can release an act of reflection that makes the feeling itself objective. The experience "terminates" in this act of reflection just as in a volition or bodily expression. We usually say   <59> that reflection weakens feeling and that the reflecting man is incapable of intense feelings. This inference is completely unjustified. The feeling "terminates" in "passionate" expression just as in "cool" reflection. The type of expression signifies nothing about the intensity of the feeling expressed.

So far, we can conclude that feeling by its nature demands expression. The various types of expression are various essential possibilities.[74] Feelings and expression are related by nature and meaning, not causally. The bodily expression, like other possible forms issuing from feeling and its meaning, is therefore also definitely experienced. For I not only feel how feeling is poured into expression and "unloaded" in it, but at the same time I have this expression given in bodily perception. The smile in which my pleasure is experientially externalized is at the same time given to me as a stretching of my lips. As I live in the joy, I also experience its expression in the mode of actuality and carry out the simultaneous bodily perception in the mode of non-actuality. I am not, so to speak, conscious of it. Should I then turn my attention to the perceived change of my living body, I see it as effected through a feeling. Thus a causal connection between feeling and expression has been constituted beside the sensory unity. Expression uses psycho-physical causality to become realized in a psycho-physical individual. The experienced unity of experience and expression is taken apart in bodily perception, and expression is separated as a relatively independent phenomenon. At the same time it itself becomes productive. I can stretch my mouth so that it could be "taken for" a smile but actually not be a smile.

Similar perceptual phenomena are also seen as different phe-   <60> nomena of expression independently of the will. I blush in anger, for shame, or from exertion. In all these cases I have the same perception of my "blood rising into my face." But in one instance I experience this as an expression of anger, in another I experience the same occurrence as an expression of shame, and, again, not as an expression at all but as a causal result of exertion. We have said that it requires an observant glance to make the bodily perceived expression into an intentional object in the pregnant sense. Yet the felt expression, even though experienced in the mode of actuality, also requires a particular turning of the glance to become a comprehended object. This turning of the glance is not the transition from non-actuality to actuality that is characteristic of all non-theoretical acts and their correlates.[75]

The fact that I can objectify experienced phenomena of expression and comprehend them as expression is a further condition of the possibility of voluntarily producing them. Nevertheless, the bodily change resembling an expression is not really given as the same. The furrowing of the brow in anger and the furrowing of the brow to simulate anger are clearly distinguishable in themselves even when I pass over from bodily perception to outer perception. Since phenomena of expression appear as the outpouring of feelings, they are simultaneously the expression of the psychic characteristics they announce. For example, the furious glance reveals a vehement state of mind. We shall conclude this investigation by a consideration of experiences of will.

(e) Will and Living Body

Experiences of will also have an important meaning for the constitution of psycho-physical unity. For one thing, they are important because of accompanying physical manifestations (sensations of tension, etc.), though we shall not consider these further because we are already familiar with them from our discussion of feelings.

<61>   Other phenomena of bodily expression being considered do not appear to be the expression of volition itself, but to be feeling components of complex volitional experiences. I may sit here quietly weighing two practical possibilities. Then I have chosen, have made a decision. I plant my feet on the floor and spring up vivaciously. These movements do not express a volitional decision, but the resulting feeling of decisiveness, of activity, of unrest that fills me. Will itself is not expressed in this sense, but, like feeling, neither is it isolated in itself, having to work itself out. Just as feeling releases or motivates volition from itself (or another

possible "expression" in a wider sense), so will externalizes itself in action. To act is always to produce what is not present. The "fieri" of what is willed conforms to the "fiat!" of the volitional decision and to the "facere" of the subject of the will in action. This action can be physical. I can decide to climb a mountain and carry out my decision. It seems that the action is called forth entirely by the will and is fulfilling the will. But the action as a whole is willed, not each step. I will to climb the mountain. What is "necessary" for this takes care "of itself." The will employs a psycho-physical mechanism to fulfill itself, to realize what is willed, just as feeling uses such a mechanism to realize its expression.

At the same time the control of the mechanism or at least the "switching on of the machine" is experienced. It may be experienced step by step if it means overcoming a resistance at the same time. If I become tired halfway up, this causes a resistance to the movement to seize my feet and they stop serving my will. Willing and striving oppose each other and fight for control of the organism. Should the will become master, then every step may now be willed singly and the effective movement experienced by overcoming the countereffect.

The same thing applies in purely psychic domains. I decide to take an examination and almost automatically do the required preparation. Or my strength may give out before I reach my goal, and I must call to life each requisite mental act by a volition to overcome a strong resistance. The will is thus master of the soul <62> as of the living body, even though not experienced absolutely nor without the soul refusing obedience. The world of objects disclosed in experience sets a limit to the will. The will can turn toward an object that is perceived, felt, or otherwise given as being present, but it cannot comprehend an object not present. This does not mean that the world of objects itself is beyond the range of my will. I can bring about a change in the world of objects but I cannot deliberately bring about its perception if it itself is not present. The will is further limited by countereffective tendencies which are themselves in part body-bound (when they are caused by sensory feelings) and in part not.

Is this effect of willing and tending on the soul and on the living body psycho-physical causality or is it that much-talked-about causality in freedom, the severing of the "continuous" chain of causality? Action is always the creation of what is not. This process can be carried out in causal succession, but the initiation of the process, the true intervention of the will is not experienced as causal but as a special effect. This does not mean that the will has nothing to do with causality. We find it causally conditioned when we feel how a tiredness of body prevents a volition from prevailing. The will is causally effective when we feel a victorious will overcome the tiredness, even making it disappear. The will's fulfillment is also linked to causal conditions, since it carries out all its effects through a causally regulated instrument. But what is truly creative about volition is not a causal effect. All these causal relationships are external to the essence of the will. The will disregards them as soon as it is no longer the will of a psycho-physical individual and yet will. Tending also has a similar structure, and action progressing from a tendency does not appear as a

<63> causal succession, either. The difference is that in tending the "I" is drawn into the action, does not step into it freely, and no creative strength is lived out in it. Every creative act in the true sense is a volitional action. Willing and tending both have the capacity to make use of psycho-physical causality, but it can only be said that the willing "I" is the master of the living body.

5. Transition to the Foreign Individual

We have at least outlined an account of what is meant by an individual "I" or by individuals. It is a unified object inseparably joining together the conscious unity of an "I" and a physical body in such a way that each of them takes on a new character. The physical body occurs as a living body; consciousness occurs as the soul of the unified individual. This unity is documented by the fact that specific events are given as belonging to the living body and to the soul at the same time: sensations, general feelings. The causal tie between physical and psychic events and the resulting mediated causal relationship between the soul and the real outer world further document this unity. The psycho-physical individual as a whole belongs to the order of nature. The living body in contrast with the physical body is characterized by having fields of sensation, being located at the zero point of orientation of the spatial world, moving voluntarily and being constructed of moving organs, being the field of expression of the experiences of its "I" and the instrument of the "I's" will.[76] We have gotten all these characteristics from considering our own individual. Now we must show how the foreign one is structured for us.

(a) The Fields of Sensation of the Foreign Living Body   <64>

Let us begin by considering what permits the foreign living body to be comprehended as a living body, what distinguishes it from other physical bodies. First we ask how fields of sensation are given to us. As we saw, we have a primordial givenness in "bodily perception" of our own fields of sensation.[77] Moreover, they are "co-given" in the outer perception of our physical body in that very peculiar way where what is not perceived can be there itself together with what is perceived. The other's fields of sensation are there for me in the same way. Thus the foreign living body is "seen" as a living body. This kind of givenness, that we want to call "con-primordiality," confronts us in the perception of the thing.[78] The averted and interior sides of a spatial thing are co-given with its seen sides. In short, the whole thing is "seen." But, as we have already said, this givenness of the one side implies tendencies to advance to new givennesses. If we do this, then in a pregnant sense we primordially perceive the formerly averted sides that were given con-primordially.

Such fulfillment of what is intended or anticipated is also possible in the "co-seeing" of our own fields of sensation, only not in progressive outer perception, but in the transition from outer to bodily perception. The co-seeing of foreign fields of sensation also implies tendencies, but their primordial fulfillment is in principle excluded here. I can neither bring them to primordial givenness to myself in progressive outer perception nor in the transition to bodily perception. Empathic representation is the only fulfillment possible here.

Besides by empathic presentation or con-primordiality, I can also bring these fields of sensation to givenness by making them intuitive for me, not in the character of perception, but only representationally. This was delineated in the description of em-

<65> pathic acts. Fields of sensation owe the character of being "there themselves" to the animatedly given physical body with which they are given. This becomes still clearer in the consideration of actual sensations themselves instead of fields of sensation. The hand resting on the table does not lie there like the book beside it. It "presses" against the table more or less strongly; it lies there limpid or stretched; and I "see" these sensations of pressure and tension in a con-primordial way. If I follow out the tendencies to fulfillment in this "co-comprehension," my hand is moved (not in reality, but "as if") to the place of the foreign one. It is moved into it and occupies its position and attitude, now feeling its sensations, though not primordially and not as being its own. Rather, my own hand feels the foreign hand's sensation "with," precisely through the empathy whose nature we earlier differentiated from our own experience and every other kind of representation. During this projection, the foreign hand is continually perceived as belonging to the foreign physical body so that the empathized sensations are continually brought into relief as foreign in contrast with our own sensations. This is so even when I am not turned toward this contrast in the manner of awareness.

(b) The Conditions of the Possibility of Sensual Empathy

The possibility of sensual empathy ("a sensing-in," we should say to be exact) is warranted by the interpretation of our own living body as a physical body and our own physical body as a living body because of the fusion of outer and bodily perception.[79] It is also warranted by the possibility of spatially altering

<66> this physical body, and finally by the possibility of modifying its real properties in fantasy while retaining its type. Were the size of my hand, such as its length, width, span, etc. given to me as inalterably fixed, the attempt at empathy with any hand having different properties would have to fail because of the contrast between them. But actually empathy is also quite successful with men's and children's hands which are very different from mine,

for my physical body and its members are not given as a fixed type but as an accidental realization of a type that is variable within definite limits. On the other hand, I must retain this type. I can only empathize with physical bodies of this type; only them can I interpret as living bodies.

This is not yet an unequivocal limitation. There are types of various levels of generality to which correspond various possible levels of empathy. The type "human physical body" does not define the limits of the range of my empathic objects, more exactly, of what can be given to me as a living body. However, it certainly marks off a range within which a very definite degree of empathic fulfillment is possible. In the case of empathy with the foreign hand, fulfillment, though perhaps not "adequate," is yet possible and very extensive. What I sense non-primordially can coincide exactly with the other's primordial sensation. Should I perhaps consider a dog's paw in comparison with my hand, I do not have a mere physical body, either, but a sensitive limb of a living body. And here a degree of projection is possible, too. For example, I may sense-in pain when the animal is injured. But other things, such as certain positions and movements, are given to me only as empty presentations without the possibility of fulfillment. And the further I deviate from the type "human being" the smaller does the number of possibilities of fulfillment become.

The interpretation of foreign living bodies as of my type helps make sense out of the discussion of "analogizing" in comprehending another. Of course, this analogizing has very little to do with "inferences by analogy." "Association by similarity" also turns out to be the comprehension of a single instance of a familiar type. Volkelt, along with others, emphasizes this as important for empathy.[80] In order to understand a movement, for example, <67> a gesture of pride, I must first "link" it to other similar movements familiar to me. According to our interpretation, this means that I must find a familiar type in it.[81] This discussion offers themes for extended investigations. We must satisfy ourselves with the foregoing as an indication of the "transcendental" questions arising, since we cannot allow ourselves a more detailed discussion.

(c) The Consequence of Sensual Empathy and Its Absence in the
Literature on Empathy Under Discussion

At the end of the empathic process, in our case as well as
usually, there is a new objectification where we find the "perceiving hand" facing us as at the beginning. (To be sure, it is present
the whole time—in contrast with progression in outer perception—only not in the mode of attention.) Now, however, it has a
new dignity because what was presented as empty has found its
fulfillment. Thanks to the fact that sensations essentially belong
to an "I," there is already a foreign "I" given together with the
constitution of the sensual level of the foreign physical body
(which, strictly speaking, we may now no longer call a "physical
body"). This "I" can become conscious of itself, even though it is
not necessarily "awake."

As we already noted, this basic level of constitution has always
been ignored so far. Volkelt goes into "sensing-in" in various
ways, but he briefly characterizes it as the reproduction of sensation and does not explore its own essence. Neither does he consider its meaning for the constitution of the individual, only considering it as an aid to the occurrence of what he alone designates
as empathy. This is the empathizing of feelings and especially of
<68>   moods. He does not want to call sensation empathy because, if
empathy stopped at sensations, it would be "something frankly
pitiful and lamentable." We do not want to impute this to empathy by any means. On the other hand, our preceding demonstrations show that sensations cannot be assessed quite so narrowly.
Finally, emotional reasons should not cause us to separate what
essentially belongs together. The comprehension of foreign experiences—be they sensations, feelings, or what not—is a unified, typical, even though diversely differentiated modification of
consciousness and requires a uniform name. Therefore, we have
selected the already customary term "empathy" for some of these
phenomena. Should one desire to retain this for the narrower
domain, then he must coin a new expression for the broader one.

In one place Lipps contrasts sensations with feelings. He says
that I look at the man who is cold, not at the sensation of coldness,
but at the discomfort he feels. It is reflection that first concludes

that this discomfort arises from sensations. We can easily see how Lipps arrives at this contention. It is implied by his one-sided focusing on the "symbol," the phenomenon of "expression." Only those experiences expressed by a countenance, a gesture, etc. are given to him as "visible" or intuitive. And sensations are certainly not expressed actually. However, it is certainly a strong contention that they are thus not given to us directly at all, but only as the basic support of states of feeling. He who does not see that another is cold by his "goose flesh" or his blue nose, having first to consider that this discomfort he feels is indeed a "chilliness," must be suffering from striking anomalies of interpretation. Furthermore, this chilly discomfort need not be based on sensations of coldness at all. For example, it can also occur as the psychic accompanying appearance of a state of excitement. On the other hand, I can very well "be cold without being cold," i.e., can have sensations of coldness without feeling the least bit uncomfortable. Thus we would have a badly-appointed acquaintance with foreign sensations if we could only reach them by the detour over states of feeling based on such sensations.

(d) The Foreign Living Body as the Center of Orientation of the Spatial World

We come to the second constituent of the living body: its position at the zero point of orientation. The living body cannot be separated from the givenness of the spatial outer world. The other's physical body as a mere physical body is spatial like other things and is given at a certain location, at a certain distance from me as the center of spatial orientation, and in certain spatial relationships to the rest of the spatial world. When I now interpret it as a sensing living body and empathically project myself into it, I obtain a new image[82] of the spatial world and a new zero point of orientation. It is not that I shift my zero point to this place, for I retain my "primordial" zero point and my "primor-   <69> dial" orientation while I am empathically, non-primordially obtaining the other one. On the other hand, neither do I obtain a fantasized orientation nor a fantasized image of the spatial world. But this orientation, as well as the empathized sensations, is conprimordial, because the living body to which it refers is perceived as a physical body at the same time and because it is given primordially to the other "I," even though non-primordially to me.

This orientation takes us a long way in constituting the foreign individual, for by means of it the "I" of the sensing, living body empathizes the whole fullness of outer perception in which the spatial world is essentially constituted. A sensing subject has become one which carries out acts. And so all designations resulting from the immanent essential examination of perceptual consciousness apply to it.[83] This also makes statements about the essentially possible various modalities of the accomplishment of acts and about the actuality and non-actuality of perceptual acts and of what is perceived applicable to this subject. In principle, the outwardly perceiving "I" can perceive in the manner of the "cogito," i.e., in the mode of specific "being directed" toward an object; and, simultaneously given, is the possibility of reflection on the accomplished act. Naturally, empathy with a perceiving consciousness in general does not prescribe the form of accomplishment actually present; for this we need specific criteria according to the case. However, the essential possibilities present in particular cases are determined *a priori*.

<70>

(e) *The Foreign World Image as the Modification of Our Own World Image*

The world image I empathize in the other is not only a modification of my own image on the basis of the other orientation, it also varies with the way I interpret his living body. A person without eyes fails to have the entire optical givenness of the world.

Doubtless, a world image suiting his orientation exists. But if I ascribe it to him, I am under a gross empathic deception. The world is constituted for him only through the remaining senses, and in reality it may be impossible for me empathically to fulfill his world given in empty presentations. This is so because of my actual, life-long habits of intuiting and thinking. But these empty presentations and the lack of intuitive fulfillment are given to me. To a still greater extent this applies to a person lacking a sense who empathizes with a person having all his senses. Here emerges the possibility of enriching our own world image through another's, the significance of empathy for experiencing the real outer world. This significance is evident in still another respect.

(f) Empathy as the Condition of the Possibility of Constituting Our Own Individual

From the viewpoint of the zero point of orientation gained in empathy, I must no longer consider my own zero point as the zero point, but as a spatial point among many. By this means, and only <71> by this means, I learn to see my living body as a physical body like others. At the same time, only in primordial experience is it given to me as a living body. Moreover, it is given to me as an incomplete physical body in outer perception and as different from all others.[84] In "reiterated empathy"[85] I again interpret this physical body as a living body, and so it is that I first am given to myself as a psycho-physical individual in the full sense. The fact of being founded on a physical body is now constitutive for this psycho-physical individual. This reiterated empathy is at the same time the condition making possible that mirror-image-like givenness of myself in memory and fantasy on which we have touched several times.[86] Probably it also accounts for the interpretation of the mirror image itself, into which we shall not go more deeply. Since there is only one zero point and my physical body at that zero point given to me, there certainly is the possibility of shifting my zero point together with my physical body. A fantasized shift is also possible which then conflicts with the real zero point and its orientation (and, as we saw, this possibility is the condition of the possibility of empathy). But I cannot look at myself freely as at another physical body. If in a childhood memory or fantasy I see myself in the branch of a tree or on the shore of the Bosporus, I see myself as another or as another sees me. This makes empathy possible for me. But its significance extends still further.

(g) The Constitution of the Real Outer World in Intersubjective Experience

The world I glimpse in fantasy is a non-existing world because of its conflict with my primordial orientation. Nor do I need to bring this non-existence to givenness as I live in fantasy. The world I glimpse empathically is an existing world, posited as hav-

<72>   ing being like the world primordially perceived. The perceived world and the world given empathically are the same world differently seen. But it is not only the same one seen from different sides as when I perceive primordially and, traversing continuous varieties of appearances, go from one standpoint to another. Here each earlier standpoint motivates the later one, each following one severs the preceding one. Of course, I also accomplish the transition from my standpoint to the other's in the same manner, but the new standpoint does not step into the old one's place. I retain them both at the same time. The same world is not merely presented now in one way and then in another, but in both ways at the same time. And not only is it differently presented depending on the momentary standpoint, but also depending on the nature of the observer. This makes the appearance of the world dependent on individual consciousness, but the appearing world—which is the same, however and to whomever it appears—is made independent of consciousness. Were I imprisoned within the boundaries of my individuality, I could not go beyond "the world as it appears to me." At least it would be conceivable that the possibility of its independent existence, that could still be given as a possibility, would always be undemonstrable. But this possibility is demonstrated as soon as I cross these boundaries by the help of empathy and obtain the same world's second and third appearance which are independent of my perception. Thus empathy as the basis of intersubjective experience becomes the condition of possible knowledge of the existing outer world, as Husserl[87] and also Royce[88] present it.

Now we can also take a position on other attempts at constituting the individual in the literature on empathy. We see that Lipps is completely justified in maintaining that our own individual, as well as the multiplicity of "I's", occurs on the basis of the perception of foreign physical bodies in which we come upon a conscious life by the mediation of empathy. We first actually consider our-
<73>   selves as an individual, as "one 'I' among many," when we have learned to consider ourselves by "analogy" with another. This theory is inadequate because he is content with such a brief indication. He held the foreign individual's physical body in the one

hand and his single experiences in the other. In addition, he limited them to what is given in "symbolic relation," and then he stopped. He neither showed how these two get together nor demonstrated empathy's part in constituting the individual.

We can also discuss our theory in terms of Münsterberg's interpretation[89] to which we really did not find an approach earlier. If we understand him correctly, he concludes that we have side by side and separate, on the one hand, the other subject's acts given in co-experiencing and on the other hand foreign physical bodies and the spatial world given to them in a specific constellation. (Münsterberg calls this world "idea" [*Vorstellung*], a view we cannot take time to refute here). When other subjects approach me with the content of statements and this content appears to be dependent on the position of their physical bodies in the spatio-temporal world, then they and their acts are first bound to their physical bodies. On the basis of our modest demonstrations, we must reject this ingenious theory as an untenable construction. Merely considered as such, a physical body could never be interpreted as the "principle of the organization" of other subjects. On the other hand, if there were no possibility of empathy, of transferring the self into the other's orientation, their statements about their phenomenal world would always have to remain unintelligible, at least in the sense of a complete fulfilling understanding in contrast with the mere empty understanding of words. Statements can fill the breach and supplement where empathy fails. Possibly they may even serve as points of departure for further empathy. But in principle they cannot substitute for empathy. Rather, their production assumes that of empathy. Finally, even if arriving at the idea of a grouping of the spatial world around a particular physical body on the basis of mere statements and the undertaking of a coordination of the subject of these <74> statements with this physical body were conceivable, it would not be clear at all how one gets from this to a phenomenon of the unified psycho-physical individual. And this we now certainly incontestably have. Naturally, this theory applies just as little to interpreting our own living body as a physical body on whose "situation" depends the "content of our ideas."

(h) The Foreign Living Body as the Bearer of Voluntary Movement

We have become acquainted with the foreign living body as the bearer of fields of sensation and as the center of orientation of the spatial world. Now we find that voluntary movement is another constituent of it. An individual's movements are not given to us as merely mechanical movements. Of course, there are also cases of this kind just as in our own movements. If I grasp and raise one hand with the other, the former's movement is given to me as mechanical in the same sense as a physical body I lift. The simultaneous sensations constitute the consciousness of a positional change of my living body, but not of the experience of "I move." On the contrary, I experience this in the other hand, and, furthermore, not only its spontaneous movement, but also how it imparts this to the hand that is moved. Since this spontaneous movement is also interpreted as a mechanical movement outwardly perceived, as well as the same movement, as we already saw, it is also "seen" as a spontaneous movement. The difference between "alive" and "mechanical" movement here intersects with "spontaneous" and "associated movement." Perhaps one is not to be reduced to the other. This intersection is evident, since each "alive" movement is also mechanical at the same time. On the other hand, spontaneous movement is not the same as living spontaneous movement, since there is also mechanical spontaneous movement. For example, suppose a rolling ball strikes another and "takes it along" in its movement. Here we have the phenomenon of mechanical spontaneous and associated movement.

<75>

Now what about the question of whether there is also alive associated movement? I believe this must be denied. Suppose I take a ride in a train or let someone push me on the ice without making sliding movements myself. If we neglect all that is not associated movement, this movement is only given to me in changing appearances of the spatial environment. It could be interpreted equally well as the movement of the landscape or as movement of my physical body. Thus, there are the familiar "optical illusions": trees and telegraph poles flying past, the stage trick in which going along a road is simulated by moving the scenery, etc. Associated movement can thus only be interpreted as mechanical and never as alive. Consequently, every alive movement seems to be a spontaneous movement.

However, we must still distinguish "imparted" movement from associated movement. We have the phenomenon of an imparted mechanical movement when a rolling ball does not "take along" a resting one, but "imparts" to it a movement of its own by its impulse (possibly stopping itself). Now, we can perceive such an imparted movement not only as mechanical, but also experience it as alive. This, however, is not an experience of "I move," but of "being moved." If someone shoves me and I fall or am hurled down an embankment, I experience the movement as alive, but not as "active." It issues from an "impulse," though it is "passive" or imparted.

Movements analogous to our own are found in foreign movements. If I see someone ride past in a car, in principle his movement appears no differently to me than the "static" parts of the car. It is mechanical associated movement and is not empathized, but outwardly perceived. Of course, I must keep his interpretation of this movement completely separate. I represent this to myself empathically when I transfer myself into his orientation. The case is entirely different if, for example, he raises himself up in the car. I "see" a movement of the type of my spontaneous movement. I interpret it as his spontaneous movement. As I participate in the movement empathically in the way already sufficiently familiar, I follow out the "co-perceived" spontaneous <76> movement's tendency to fulfillment. Finally, I objectify it so that the movement faces me as the other individual's movement.

This is how the foreign living body with its organs is given to me as able to move. And voluntary mobility is closely linked with the other constituents of the individual. In order to empathize alive movement in this physical body, we must already have interpreted it as a living body. We would never interpret the spontaneous movement of a physical body as alive, even should we perhaps illustrate its difference from imparted or associated movement to ourselves by a quasi-empathy. For example, we may "inwardly participate in" the movement of knocked and knocking ball. The character of the ball otherwise prohibits the attribution of represented alive movement to it.[90]

On the other hand, rigid immobility conflicts with the phenomenon of the sensitive living body and the living organism in general.[91] We cannot imagine a completely immobile living being. That which is bound to one place completely motionless is "turned to stone." So far, spatial orientation cannot be completely separated from voluntary mobility. First of all, the varieties of perception would become so limited if spontaneous movement ceased that the constitution of a spatial world (so far, the individual one) would become dubious. This abolishes the possibility of transference into the foreign living body and so of a fulfilling empathy and the gaining of his orientation. Thus voluntary movement is a part of the structure of the individual and is entirely nonsuspendable.

<77>   *(i) The Phenomena of Life*

Now let us consider a group of phenomena that participate in the structure of the individual in a special way: they appear in the living body and also as psychic experiences. I would like to call them the specific phenomena of life. They include growth, development and aging, health and sickness, vigor and sluggishness (general feelings, in our terms, or, as Scheler would say, "feeling ourselves to be in our living body"). As he has protested against empathy in general, Scheler has very particularly protested against "explaining" phenomena of life by empathy.[92] He would be entirely justified if empathy were a genetic process so that the elucidation of this tendency explained away what it was to elucidate, as we mentioned earlier. Otherwise, I see no possibility of detaching the phenomena of life from the individual's other constituents or of exhibiting anything but an empathic comprehension of them.

In considering general feelings as our own experience, we have seen how they "fill" the living body and the soul, how they definitely color every spiritual act and every bodily event, how they are then "co-seen" at the living body just as fields of sensation are. Thus, by his walk, posture, and his every movement, we also "see" "how he feels," his vigor, sluggishness, etc. We bring this co-intended foreign experience to fulfillment by carrying it out with him empathically. Furthermore, we not only see such vigor and sluggishness in people and animals, but also in plants. Empathic fulfillment is also possible here. Of course, what I comprehend in this case is a considerable modification of my own life. A plant's general feeling does not appear as the coloring of its acts, for there is no basis at all to believe such acts are present. Neither do I have any right to ascribe an "awake" "I" to the plant, nor a reflective consciousness of its feelings of life. Even the otherwise familiar constituents of animals are absent. It is at least doubtful whether the plant has sensations,[93] and so our empathy is unjusti-   <78> fied if we believe we are inflicting pain on a tree by cutting it down with an ax. A plant is not the center of orientation of the spatial world either, nor voluntarily mobile, even though it is capable of alive movement in contrast with the inorganic. On the other hand, the absence of this constitution does not justify us in interpreting what is present in a new way and distinguishing the phenomena of life in plants from our own. I would not like to offer an opinion on whether we should look at the phenomena of life as essentially psychic or only as an essential basis for psychic existence [*Daseins*].[94] That phenomena of life have an experiential character in psychic contexts is hardly contestable.

Now perhaps someone will think that I have selected general feeling as a very convenient example of the psychic nature of phenomena of life. However, this psychic nature must also be demonstrable in other phenomena of life. Scheler has himself directed us to the "experience of life."[95] First calling "lived," isolated, finished experiences "psychic," as he does, seems to me like a definition not derived from the essence of the psychic. The psychic entity present (the primordial one, according to us) is what is becoming, is experience. What became, was lived, and is finished sinks back into the stream of the past. We leave it behind us when we step into new experience; it loses its primordiality but remains the "same experience." First it is alive and then dead, but not first non-psychic and then psychic. (There is no positive term for "non-psychic.") Just as solidifying wax is first liquid and then hard but still wax, so the same material body remains. There is no non-psychic individual experience. (The pure experience of the reduction is non-psychic when it becomes as well as when it became.) Soul is not to be separated from life.

<79> Scheler has emphasized that there is an experience of life ascension and one of life decline.[96] This is an experience and not an objective possession or the verification of discernible stages of development. The continuum of life itself is given to us as such and not as a composite of stretches connecting high points. Furthermore, the ascension to these points, the development and not only its results, is given to us. (Of course, in order to perceive the result, we must first "become conscious of" this development, i.e., make it objective. For example, we become conscious of our strength waning when we notice we are weak. Correspondingly, in "higher psychic life" we become conscious of an inclination disappearing when we find it no longer present, etc.) Nor is it a mere metaphor to compare our development with that of a plant; it is a genuine analogy in the previously defined sense of comprehending that something belongs to the same type.

Bodily "states" are no different: "feeling sick" has little to do with "pain." For instance, one can feel very healthy with a painful bodily injury such as a broken arm with complications, etc. One can also feel very ill without pain. I look at this "state" in the other and bring it to givenness to myself in empathic projection. The attentive observer sees a variety of single traits in the whole disease picture which remain hidden from the fleeting glance. This is what the "schooled view" of the physician has over the lay person. The diagnosis he makes on the basis of this picture is no longer made thanks to empathy, but thanks to his knowledge that this "clinical picture" is an effect of the cause in question. Thus he thinks he "sees" carcinoma by yellow, sunken cheeks, or he sees tuberculosis by the red spots and unnatural gleam of the eyes. But this clinical picture itself, this distinguishing of the variety of types of illnesses on which all diagnosis is based, is yielded to him by his talent for empathy cultivated by focusing on this group of

<80> phenomena and by long practice in extensive differentiation. Of course, this empathy mostly ceases at the first introductory level, not proceeding to projection into the ill condition. And the physician's relationship to his patients, with whose welfare he is en-

trusted, is no different from the gardener's relationship to his plants, whose thriving he oversees. He sees them full of fresh strength or ailing, recovering or dying. He elucidates their condition for himself empathically. In terms of cause, he looks for the cause of the condition and finds ways to influence it.

(k) Causality[97] in the Structure of the Individual

Again, the possibility of such causal reflection is based on empathy. The foreign individual's physical body as such is given as a part of physical nature in causal relationships with other physical objects. He who pushes it imparts motion to it; its shape can be changed by blows and pressure; different illumination changes its color, etc. But these causal relationships are not all. As we know, the foreign physical body is not seen as a physical body, but as a living one. We see it suffer and carry out effects other than the physical. Pricking a hand is not the same as pounding a nail into a wall, even though it is the same procedure mechanically, namely, driving in a sharp object. The hand senses pain if stuck, and we see this. We must disregard this artificially and reduce this phenomenon in order to see what it has in common with the other one. We "see" this effect because we see the hand as sensitive, because we project ourselves into it empathically and so interpret every physical influence on it as a "stimulus" evoking a psychic response.

Along with these effects of outer causes, we comprehend effects within the individual himself. For example, we may see a child actively romping about and then becoming tired and cross. <81> We then interpret tiredness and the bad mood as the effects of movement. We have already seen how movements come to givenness for us as alive movements and how tiredness comes to givenness. As we shall soon see, we also comprehend the "bad mood" empathically. Now, we may not infer the causal sequence from the data obtained, but also experience it empathically. For example, we comprehend interpsychic causality similarly when we observe the process of contagion of feelings in others while we ourselves are immune to the infectious material. Perhaps when the actor says, "You can hear nothing but sobbing and women weeping," we perceive a suppressed sob in all parts of the audience. And, projecting ourselves into this soul-stirring spirit, we become seized by the mood portrayed. In this way we get an image of the causal process being enacted.

Finally, we also perceive how an individual affects the outer world by every action that changes physical nature, by impulsive as well as willful ones. For example, when I observe the "reaction" to a stimulus when a stone flying toward someone is driven from its course by a "mechanical" resistance movement, I see a causal process into which psychic connecting links have been inserted. Projecting myself into the other, I interpret that object as a stimulus and experience the release of the counter-movement. (Such processes can take place unnoticed, but it is entirely unjustified to designate them as "unconscious" or as "purely physiological.") Then I experience the stone's diversion from its course as the effect of the reaction.

Suppose I see someone act on a decision of will. For example, on a bet he may pick up a heavy load and carry it. Then I empathically grasp how the action issues from a volition, here appearing as the *primum movens* of the causal process and not as a connecting link in a series of physical causes. We have the effect of the psychic on the physical given phenomenally and also the psychic on the psychic without the mediation of a physical connecting link. This latter is so, for example, in the case of conta-
<82> gion of feeling not caused by a bodily expression, even if it is mediated by a form of expression to make interpretation of the experience possible.[98] But whether or not this effect is physically mediated or purely psychic, it certainly has the same structure as phenomenal causal relationships in physical nature.

Now Scheler is of the opinion, in agreement with Bergson, that there is an entirely new kind of causality in the psychic domain not existing in the physical domain.[99] This new kind of efficacy is to consist of the fact that every past experience can in principle have an effect on every future one without mediating connecting links, thus without being reproduced, either. Also coming events can affect present experience. In a broader sense, he says that psychic causality is not dependent on a limitation of every experience by what went before. Rather, in its dependence on the totality of experience, it depends on the individual's entire life. In the first place, if we were to stick to the last formulation, we would have to completely accept the fact that every experience is conditioned by the entire series of previous experiences. But we would also have to accept that every physical occurrence is conditioned by the entire chain of causality. The fundamental difference here is that "the same causes have the same effects" in the physical domain while in the psychic domain it can be shown that the appearance of the "same causes" is essentially excluded. But he who strictly supports the relationship of causing to caused experience could hardly demonstrate a new kind of efficacy.

Let us try to make this clear by examples of what we have in mind.[100] A deliberate decision on a problem put to me continues to direct the course of my action long after the actual decision without my being "conscious" of this as present in current action. Does this mean that an isolated past experience determines my present experience from that time on? Not at all. This volition that remained unfulfilled for a long time has not fallen "into forgottenness" during this time, has not sunk back into the stream of the past, become "lived life" in Scheler's terms. It has only gone out of the mode of actuality over into that of non-actuality, out of activity into passivity. Part of the nature of consciousness is that the cogito, the act in which the "I" lives, is surrounded by a marginal zone of background experiences in each moment of experience. These are non-actualities no longer or not yet cogito and therefore not accessible to reflection, either. In order to be comprehended, they must first pass through the form of the cogito, which they can do at any time. They are still primordially present, even if not actually, and therefore have efficacy. The unfulfilled volition is not dead, but continues to live in the background of consciousness until its time comes and it can be realized. Then its effect begins. Thus, it is not something past which affects the present, but something that reaches into the present. Therefore, we quite agree that a reproduction of the volition does not set the action in motion. And, indeed, we will go even further and say that volition would not be in a position to do this at all. A forgotten volition cannot have an effect, and a "reproduced" volition is not an alive one, either, but a represented one. As such it is unable to affect any behavior (as little as

<83>

in a dark room we can produce the fantasy of a burning lamp to provide the necessary light for reading). It must first be relived, lived through again, in order to be able to have an effect.

Future events which "throw their shadows in advance" are no different. Scheler gives an example from James[101] who, under the influence of an unpleasant logic course he had to teach afternoons, undertook many unnecessary activities the entire day before simply so that he would find no time for the burdensome preparation. Yet he did not "think about it." Every expectation of a threatening event is of this type. We turn our attention to another object to escape the fear, but it does not vanish. Rather, it remains "in the background" and influences our entire conduct. As a non-actual experience not specifically directed, this fear has its object in the expected event. This is not completely present, but constantly tends toward going over into actual experience, toward pulling the "I" into itself. The fear constantly resists giving itself to this cogito. Its rescue is in other actual experiences that are still blocked in their pure course by that background experience.

<84>

And of what finally concerns the efficacy of the whole life on every moment of its existence [*Daseins*] we must say: Everything living into the present can have an effect, irrespective of how far the initiation of the affecting experience is from "now." Experiences of early childhood can also endure into my present, even though pushed into the background by the profusion of later events. This can be clearly seen in dispositions toward other persons. I do not "forget" my friends when I am not thinking of them. They then belong to the unnoticed present horizon of my world. My love for them is living even when I am not living in it. It influences my actual feeling and conduct. Out of love for someone, I can abstain from activities which would cause displeasure without "being conscious" of this. Likewise, animosity against a person, inculcated into me in my childhood, can make an impression on my later life. This is true even though this animosity is pushed entirely into the background and I do not think of this person at all any more. Then, when I meet the animosity again, it can go over into actuality and be discharged in an action or else be brought to reflective clarity and so be made ineffectual. On the contrary, what belongs to my past, what is temporarily or permanently forgotten and can only come to givenness to me in the character of representation by reminiscence or by another's account, has no effect on me. A remembered love is not a primordial feeling and cannot influence me. If I do someone a favor because of a past preference, this inclination is based on a positive opinion of this past preference, not on the represented feeling.   <85>

All that has been said shows that the cases Scheler brings up do not prove that there is a difference in the phenomenal structure of efficacy in the physical and in the psychic domains. We have not found a "long-range effect" in the psychic domain. And in the domain of mechanical causality, we also have a parallel accumulation of latent strength and an effectiveness of hidden strength such as we have found here. For example, accumulated electrical energy first "affects" at the moment of discharge.

Finally, we also have analogous circumstances in bodily processes. The appearance of illness is preceded by an "incubation period" in which the cause gives no indication of its presence by any effect. On the other hand, one can ascertain numerous changes in an organism long before one can find their cause. In spite of the similarity of the causal phenomenon, we cannot here deny profound differences between physical and psychic causality. Yet, to demonstrate this we need an exact study of the dissimilar structure of psychic and physical reality.

(l) The Foreign Living Body as the Bearer of Phenomena of Expression

We have become acquainted with the foreign living body as the bearer of a psychic life that we "look at" in a certain way. Now there is still a group of phenomena that disclose a further domain of the psyche to us in a peculiarly characterized way. When I "see" shame "in" blushing, irritation in the furrowed brow, anger in the clenched fist, this is a still different phenomenon than when I look at the foreign living body's level of sensation or perceive the other individual's sensations and feelings of life with him. In the latter case I comprehend the one with the other. In the former case I see the one through the other. In the new phenomenon what is psychic is not only co-perceived with what is

bodily but expressed through it. The experience and its expres-
<86> sion are related in a way we find portrayed by Fr. Th. Vischer and
especially by Lipps as the symbolic relationship.[102]
    Let us make clear the different viewpoints on this problem
which Lipps took at different times. In the first edition of
Ethischen Grundfragen (1899) he says that the externalizations of
life are signs which become significant because they awaken in us
memories of our own experiences.[103] In his writings since 1903—
in both volumes of *Asthetik I*, in *Leitfaden*, from the very first
edition on, in the new edition of *Ethischen Grundfragen*, and in
other shorter writings—he strongly contests this description and
energetically rejects the interpretation of life externalizations as
"signs."
    In the meantime, Husserl's *Logische Untersuchungen* appears.
The first investigation sets forth the relationship between word
and meaning, that there are phenomenal unities which cannot be
made at all intelligible by allusions to an association. These expositions could have stimulated Lipps to revise his views. From then
on he distinguishes between "sign" and "expression" or "symbol." To say that something is a sign means that something perceived says to me that something else exists. Thus smoke is a sign
of fire. Symbol means that in something perceived there is something else and, indeed, we co-comprehend something psychic in
it. He also used "co-experienced" here. An example which Lipps
likes to bring up for the "symbolic relation" may elucidate the
difference. How are sadness and a sad countenance related on the
<87> one hand, and fire and smoke on the other? Both cases[104] have
something in common: An object of outer perception leads to
something not perceived in the same way. However, there is a
different kind of givenness present. The smoke indicating fire to
me is my "theme," the object of my actual turning-toward, and
awakens in me tendencies to proceed in a further context. Interest flows off in a specific direction. The transition from one
theme to another is carried out in the typical motivational form
of: If the one is, then the other is, too. (There is already more
present here than mere association. The smoke reminds me of
fire, even though this may also lead us to association.) Sadness
"being-co-given" in the sad countenance is something else. The

sad countenance is actually not a theme that leads over to another one at all, but it is at one with sadness. This occurs in such a way that the countenance itself can step entirely into the background. The countenance is the outside of sadness. Together they form a natural unity.

The difference also becomes clear in single cases where there are actually experiences of the indicator type given. I notice a familiar facial expression in a close acquaintance and determine that, when he looks like that, he is in a bad mood. But such cases are deviations from the normal case, that of symbolic givenness. Moreover, they already presume a certain symbolic givenness.[105] The indication and the symbol both point beyond themselves without wanting to or having to. (As we shall see, this distinguishes them both from the genuine sign.)

There are differences, however. If I remain turned toward the smoke and observe how it rises and disperses, this is no less "natural" than if I go over to the fire. Should I think of the tendencies leading me in this direction as gone, then I certainly no longer have the full perceptual object, but still the same object, an object of the same kind. On the contrary, should I consider the sad countenance as a mere distortion of face, I do not have the same <88> object at all any more nor even an object of the same kind. This is related to the difference of the possibilities of empathy in both cases. In one case what is presented as empty is fulfilled in progressive outer perception and in the other through a here necessary μετάβασις εἰς ἄλλο γένος, the transition to empathic projection. The relationship between what is perceived and what is presented as empty proves to be an experienceable, intelligible one. It can also be that the symbol does not yet point in a specific direction. Then it is still a pointer into emptiness so that what I see is incomplete. There is more to it, but I just do not know what yet.

These expositions should make clear what Lipps means by symbol. But this still does not mean that whatever he interprets as a symbol is really a symbol, and that we already have a sufficient distinction between "indication" and "symbol." Symbols for him are gestures, movements, resting forms, natural sounds, and words. Since he openly uses "gestures" here for involuntary externalizations, his designation proves correct. The description certainly does not cover purposeful externalizations. This gets us into the sphere of signs.

For the present I would like to neglect "resting forms" such as facial features, the shape of the hand, etc.—the "expressions of personality"—and confine myself to the expression of actual experiences. Thus movements in which there is presumed to lie a "kind of inner activity" or a "manner of feeling" can have various meanings here. The whole outer habitus of a person, his manner of movement and his posture, can indicate something of his personality. This would be dealt with in "resting forms" and can be omitted here. Further, Lipps thinks that a movement can appear as light, free, and elastic or as clumsy and restricted. This belongs among the phenomena of life whose givenness we have already considered. Finally, other feelings can also be co-comprehended together with movements. For example, I can see a person's sadness by his gait and posture. However, a symbolic relation is not present here, but an indicator. The movement is not sad in the same way that the countenance is sad. The sadness is not expressed in the movement. On the contrary, emotional expressions are on exactly the same plane as visible movements of expression. Fear is at one with the cry of fear just as sadness is with the countenance. The givenness of fear differs from the givenness of the car only indicated to me by the rolling of its wheels, as the givenness of sadness in the countenance differs from the givenness of fire by the smoke. And the material going into the verbal expression is closely related to emotional expressions. Cheerfulness or sorrow, calmness or excitement, friendliness or rejection can lie in the tone of the voice. Here, too, a symbolic relation is present, yet the relationship is veiled by what is due to the word as such. However, it is a complete mistake to designate the word itself as a symbol, to contend that there is an act of interpretation in the speaker's statement of the act of judgment, as sadness is in his countenance, to contend that the comprehension of speech is based on this.[106]

In order to show this, we need a more detailed investigation of the givenness of the word (that is heard and understood). At the same time we can discuss the nature of the sign in general, of

<89>

which we have already spoken frequently. For example, signs are the signals of ships or the flag announcing that the king is in the castle. Like signals, verbal expressions are not themes themselves, but only the intermediate points to the theme, namely, to that which they designate. They arouse a tendency to transition that is restricted if they themselves are made into themes. In the normal case of comprehension (especially of the word), the transition is so momentary that one can hardly speak of a tendency. However, the tendency becomes visible when one is stopped by a foreign word not understood at first but only containing a hint of its meaning.

What is "sensually perceived" completely recedes in the sign. This distinguishes it from the indication that becomes a "theme" in its full factual content. On the other hand, the sign is not to be put on the same plane as the symbol, for that signified is certainly not co-perceived like that comprehended in the symbol. There is <90> something more. The signal has a moment of ought, a demand in itself, finally fulfilled in the idea of him who has determined it as a sign. Every signal is stipulated as convention and determined by someone for someone. This is lost in the pure symbol. The sad countenance "ought" not to mean sadness, nor blushing shame. Symbolic and signal character are combined in a certain way in the purposeful externalization using the symbol as a sign. I now not only comprehend disapproval in the furrowed brow but it intends to and ought to announce it. The comprehended intention gives the whole phenomenon a new character. Nevertheless, the intention itself can still be given in a symbolic relation, perhaps in a glance, or it can be the result of the situation as a whole.

Now what about the word? Does this also have a moment of ought as the signal does? Apparently the word can be there as communicated and, even further, as communicated to me or to another, or as merely "thought aloud." For the present we can ignore how the word has these characteristics. At any rate, they are irrelevant to the intelligibility of the word. The words "Something is burning" mean the same thing to me when they are merely called out as when they are directed to me or to another. Indeed, nothing of these differences needs to be co-given at all. Part of their givenness is certainly that someone is speaking them, but the speaker is not comprehended in the words. Rather, he is comprehended at the same time as they. Nor does this at first play any role in the words' meaning, but only when it points toward their intuitive fulfillment. For example, in order to fulfill the meaning of a perceptual statement, I must put myself into the speaker's orientation. Thus the words can be considered entirely in themselves without regarding the speaker and all that is going on in him.

Now what distinguishes the word from the signal? On the one hand, we have the signaling thing, the circumstances of the process, the bridge that convention has thrown between them and that is perceivable as this "ought to indicate." The circumstances themselves remain entirely undisturbed by the fact that the signal <91> designates them. On the other hand, there is first of all no verbal physical body [*Wortkörper*] corresponding to the signaling physical body [*Signalkörper*], only a verbal living body [*Wortleib*]. The verbal expression could not exist by itself, and neither has it received the function of a sign from the outside in addition to what it is. Rather, it is always the bearer of meaning in entirely the same manner whether the meaning is really there or whether it is invented. On the contrary, the signal is real. If it is invented, its function as a sign is merely invented, too, whereas there is no such thing as an invented meaning of words. The living body and the soul of a word form a living unity, but one permitting to both a relatively independent development.[107] A signal cannot develop. Once it has received its designation it continues to convey it unchanged; and the function an act of choice has assigned to it, an act of choice can take away again. Further, it only exists by reason of a creative act completed in it. But as soon as it exists it is severed and independent from this act like any product of human artistry. It can be destroyed and cease functioning without its "creator" knowing anything about it. If a storm washes away all trail markers in the Riesengebirge, hikers will get lost. This can happen without the Riesengebirge Association, the creator of this system of signs, being responsible for this, since it believes they are still in the best condition. This cannot happen with a word, for it is always borne by a consciousness (which is naturally not that of him who is speaking here and now). It lives "by the grace" of a spirit (i.e., not by reason of the spirit's creative act, but in living dependence on it). The word's bearer can be an individual subject but also a group of possibly changing subjects bound into one by a continuity of experience. Finally, we have the main difference: Words point to the object through the medium of meaning, while the signal has no meaning at all but only the function of being significant. And words do not simply point to the circumstances as the signal does. What goes into them is not the circumstance, but its logico-categorical formation. Words do not signify, but express, and what is expressed is no longer what it <92> was before.[108]

Naturally, this also applies when something psychic is expressed. Should someone say to me that he is sad, I understand the meaning of the words. The sadness I now know of is not an "alive one" before me as a perceptual givenness. It is probably as little like the sadness comprehended in the symbol as the table of which I hear spoken is like the other side of the table which I see. In one case I am in the apophantic sphere, the realm of propositions and meanings, in the other case in immediate intuitive contact with the objective sphere.

Meaning is always a general one. In order to comprehend the object intended right now, we always need a givenness of the intuitive basis of the meaning experiences. There is no such intermediate level between the expressed experience and the expressing bodily change. But meaning and symbol have something in common which forces them both to be called "expression" repeatedly. This is the fact that together they constitute the unity of an object, that the expression released from the connection with what is expressed is no longer the same object (in contrast with the signaling physical body), that the expression proceeds out of the experience[109] and adapts itself to the expressed material.

These relationships are present in simple form in bodily expression; they are doubled in a certain sense in verbal expression: word, meaning, object; and, correlatively, having of the object, logical intention or meaning, and linguistic designation. The function of expressing, through which I comprehend the expressed experience as the expression, is always fulfilled in the experience in which expression proceeds from what is expressed.

We have already portrayed this earlier and also used "expression" in a broadened sense.

<93>   In the case of understanding this experiencing is not primor-
dial, but empathized. Of course, we must distinguish between
verbal and bodily expression here. Understanding of a bodily
expression is based on comprehending the foreign living body
already interpreted as a living body of an "I." I project myself
into the foreign living body, carry out the experience already co-
given to me as empty with its countenance, and experience the
experience ending in this expression.

As we saw, we can neglect the speaking individual in the word. I
myself primordially comprehend the meaning of this ideal object
in the understanding transition from word to meaning. And as
long as I remain in this sphere, I do not need the foreign individual and do not have to empathically carry out his experiences with
him. An intuitive fulfillment of what is intended is also possible
through primordial experience. I can bring the circumstances of
which the statement speaks to givenness to myself. I hear the
words, "It is raining," I understand them without considering
that someone is saying them to me. And I bring this comprehension to intuitive fulfillment when I look out the window myself.
Only if I want to have the intuition on which the speaker bases his
statement and his full experience of expression, do I need empathy.

Therefore, it should be clear that one does not arrive at experience by the path leading immediately from verbal expression to
meaning, that the word, insofar as it has an ideal meaning, is not a
symbol. But suppose that there are still other ways to get to the
word. The way to get to meaning is through the pure type of the
word. Except perhaps in solitary psychic life, we always find this
word in some kind of earthly cloak, in speech, handwriting, or
print. The form can be unnoticed; but it can also push itself
forward (for example, if it does not clearly reproduce the contour
of the words). Then it draws interest to itself and at the same time
to the speaking person.[110] He appears to be externalizing or communicating words, possibly communicating to me. In the latter
<94>   case the words "ought" to point out something to me. Now they
are no longer merely the expression of something objective, but

at the same time are the externalization or the announcement of the person's meaningful act as well as of the experiences behind it, such as a perception.

Instead of in verbal expression, the transition to the speaking person and his acts can also begin in the meaning of the words. A question, a request, a command are always directed toward someone and thus refer to the relationship of the speaker to the hearer, just as all greetings do. Here the speaker's intentions substantially assist in making the words intelligible. From his viewpoint we comprehend, not what the words mean in general, but what they mean here and now.

Words cannot be designated as symbols in their informative functions, either. This is so, first of all, because they do not form the only nor the main basis for comprehending this experience; secondly, because these experiences are not comprehended in the words, but only from their viewpoint, and are also entirely differently presented from that which is symbolically given. At most one could say that in speaking the externalization of self steps into view with the same animation as an affect does in an expressive movement, but not the experiences themselves to which the speech testifies. Yet it is still worth noting that inflection and intonation are also a part of the word as an expression (the emphasis placed on the essential parts of the speech, the rising of the voice in a question, etc.) and that these characteristics can only secondarily have a function of testifying.

Naturally, these relationships could still be investigated in more detail.[111] In terms of this characterization, let us once more make clear what distinguishes symbolic givenness from the mere "being-co-given" of what is psychic considered so far. We see that we experience this proceeding of what is outwardly perceived on the level of empathic projection from what was "co-perceived" on the first level. This was missing in the cases considered earlier.   <95>
The appearance of a sensing hand does not proceed from sensations in the way that laughter proceeds from happiness. On the other hand, the proceeding is specifically different from a causal sequence. As we said earlier, there is a different relationship between shame and blushing than between exertion and blushing. While causal relationship is always announced in the form of

if . . . then, so that the givenness of one occurrence (be it psychic or physical) motivates a progression to the givenness of the other one, here the proceeding of one experience from another is experienced in purest immanence without the detour over the object sphere.

We want to call this experienced proceeding "motivation." All that is usually designated as "motivation" is a special case of this motivation: motivation of conduct by the will, of the will by a feeling. But the proceeding of expression from experience is a special case of this motivation, too. And we also understand motivation in perception (the going over from one givenness of the object to another), of which Husserl speaks,[112] in this way. Various attempts have been made to set forth motivation as the cause of what is psychic. This interpretation is untenable for, as we saw, there is also psychic causality that is clearly distinguished from motivation. On the contrary, motivation belongs essentially to the experiential sphere. There is no other such connection. We would like to designate the motivational relationship as intelligible or meaningful in contrast with the causal one. To be intelligible means nothing more than to experience the transition from one part to another within an experiential whole (not, to have objectively), and every objective, all objective meaning, resides only in experiences of this kind. An action is a unity of intelligibility or of meaning because its component experiences have an experienceable connection.

And experience and expression form an intelligible whole in the same sense. I understand an expression, while I can merely <96> bring a sensation to givenness. This leads me through the phenomenon of expression into the meaning contexts of what is psychic and at the same time gives me an important means of correcting empathic acts.

(m) The Correction of Empathic Acts

The basis for what would suspend the unity of a meaning must be a deception. When I empathize the pain of the injured in looking at a wound, I tend to look at his face to have my experience confirmed in his expression of suffering. Should I instead perceive a cheerful or peaceful countenance, I would say to myself that he must not really be having any pain, for pain in its meaning motivates unhappy feelings visible in an expression. Further testing that consists of new acts of empathy and possible inferences based on them can also lead me to another correction: the sensual feeling is indeed present but its expression is voluntarily repressed; or perhaps this person certainly feels the pain but, because his feeling is perverted, he does not suffer from it but enjoys it.

Furthermore, penetration into their meaning contexts assists me in accurately interpreting "equivocal" expressions. Whether a blush means shame, anger, or is a result of physical exertion is actually decided by the other circumstances leading me to empathize the one or the other. If this person has just made a stupid remark, the empathized motivational context is given to me immediately as follows: insight into his folly, shame, blushing. If he clenches his fist or utters an oath as he blushes, I see that he is angry. If he has just stooped or walked quickly, I empathize a causal context instead of a motivational one. This is all done immediately without a "differential diagnosis" being necessary in the individual case. I draw on other cases for comparison as little as I need, to consider which of the possible meanings of an equivocal word applies in a given context in understanding a sentence.

By the correction of the act of empathy, it becomes clear how we understand what is concealed behind a countenance, of which <97> we spoke earlier. Formerly, we distinguished the "genuine" expression as such from the "false" one. For example, the conventional laugh was distinguished from the truly amiable one, and also the animated one from the almost hardened one still retained even when the actual stimulant causing it has already died away. But I am also able to look through the "deceiving" imitated expression. If someone assures me of his interest in sincerest tones and at the same time surveys me coldly and indifferently or with insistent curiosity, I put no trust in him.

The harmony of empathy in the unity of a meaning also makes possible the comprehension of expressive appearances unfamiliar to me from my own experience and therefore possibly not experienceable at all. An outburst of anger is an intelligible, meaningful whole within which all single moments become intelligible to me, including those unfamiliar up to that point. For example, I can understand a furious laugh. Thus, too, I can understand the tail wagging of a dog as an expression of joy if its appearance and its behavior otherwise disclose such feelings and its situation warrants them.

(n) The Constitution of the Psychic Individual and Its Significance for the Correction of Empathy

But the possibility of correction goes further. I not only interpret single experiences and single–meaning contexts, but I take them as announcements of individual attributes and their bearers, just as I take my own experiences in inner perception. I not only comprehend an actual feeling in the friendly glance, but friendliness as an habitual attribute. An outburst of anger reveals a "vehement temperament" to me. In him who penetrates an intricate association I comprehend sagacity, etc. Possibly these attributes are constituted for me in a whole series of corroborating and correcting empathic acts. But having thus gotten a picture of the foreign "character" as a unity of these attributes, this itself serves me as a point of departure for the verification of further empathic acts. If someone tells me about a dishonest act <98> by a person I have recognized as honest, I will not believe him. And, as in single experiences, there are also meaning contexts among personal attributes. There are essentially congenial and essentially uncongenial attributes. A truly good man cannot be vindictive; a sympathetic person, not cruel; a candid person, not "diplomatic," etc. Thus we comprehend the unity of a character in each attribute, as we comprehend the unity of a thing in every material attribute. Therein we possess a motivation for future experiences. This is how all the elements of the individual are constituted for us in empathic acts.

(o) Deceptions of Empathy

As in every experience, deceptions are here also possible. But here, too, they can only be unmasked by the same kind of experiential acts or else by inferences finally leading back to such acts as their basis. Many instances have already shown us what sources such deceptions can have. We come to false conclusions if we empathically take our individual characteristic as a basis instead of our type.[113] Examples are: if we ascribe our impressions of color to the color–blind, our ability to judge to the child, our aesthetic receptiveness to the uncultivated. If empathy only meant this kind of interpretation of foreign psychic life, one would justifiably have to reject it, as Scheler does. But here he is confronted with what he has reproached in other theories: He has taken the case of deception as the normal case.

But, as we said, this deception can only be removed again by empathy. If I empathize that the unmusical person has my enjoyment of a Beethoven symphony, this deception will disappear as soon as I look him in the face and see his expression of deadly boredom. We can make the same error, in principle, when we   <99> infer by analogy. Here our own actual, not typical, characteristic forms the starting point, too. If I logically proceed from this, I do not reach a deception (i.e., a supposed primordial givenness of what is not actually present), but a false inference on the basis of the false premise. The result is the same in both cases: an absence of what is really present. Certainly "common sense" does not take "inference from oneself to others" as a usable means of reaching knowledge of foreign psychic life.

In order to prevent such errors and deceptions, we need to be constantly guided by empathy through outer perception. The constitution of the foreign individual is founded throughout on the constitution of the physical body. Thus the givenness in outer perception of a physical body of a certain nature is a presupposition for the givenness of a psycho-physical individual. On the other hand, we cannot take a single step beyond the physical body through outer perception alone, but, as we saw, the individual is only possible for a subject of the same type. For example, a pure "I," for which no living body of its own and no psycho-physical relationships are constituted primordially, could perhaps have all kinds of objects given, but it could not perceive animated, living bodies—living individuals. It is, of course, very difficult to decide what is here a matter of fact and what is necessary essentially. This requires its own investigation.

*(p) The Significance of the Foreign Individual's Constitution for the
Constitution of Our Own Psychic Individual*

Now, as we saw on a lower level in considering the living body
as the center of orientation, the constitution of the foreign individual was a condition for the full constitution of our own individual. Something similar is also found on higher levels. To consider
ourselves in inner perception, i.e., to consider our psychic "I" and
its attributes, means to see ourselves as we see another and as he
<100> sees us. The original naive attitude of the subject is to be absorbed
in his experience without making it into an object. We love and
hate, will and act, are happy and sad and look like it. We are
conscious of all this in a certain sense without its being comprehended, being an object. We do not meditate on it. We do not
make it into the object of our attention or even our observation.
Furthermore, we do not evaluate it nor look at it in such a way
that we can discover what kind of a "character" it manifests. On
the contrary, we do all this in regard to foreign psychic life.
Because this life is bound to the perceived physical body, it stands
before us as an object from the beginning. Inasmuch as I now
interpret it as "like mine," I come to consider myself as an object
like it. I do this in "reflexive sympathy" when I empathically
comprehend the acts in which my individual is constituted for
him. From his "standpoint," I look through my bodily expression
at this "higher psychic life" here manifested and at the psychic
attributes here revealed.

This is how I get the "image" the other has of me, more
accurately, the appearances in which I present myself to him. Just
as the same natural object is given in as many varieties of appearances as there are perceiving subjects, so I can have just as many
"interpretations" of my psychic individual as I can have interpreting subjects.[114] Of course, as soon as the interpretation is
empathically fulfilled, the reiterated empathic acts in which I
comprehend my experience can prove to be in conflict with the
primordial experience so that this empathized "interpretation" is
exposed as a deception. And, in principle, it is possible for all the
interpretations of myself with which I become acquainted to be
wrong.

But, luckily, I not only have the possibility of bringing my experience to givenness in reiterated empathy, but can also bring it to givenness primordially in inner perception. Then I have it immediately given, not mediated by its expression or by bodily appearances. Also I now comprehend my attributes primordially and not empathically. As we said, this attitude is foreign to the natural standpoint, and it is empathy that occasions it. But this is not an essential necessity. There is also the possibility of inner perception independent from this. Thus in these contexts empathy does not appear as a constituent, but only as an important aid in comprehending our own individual. This is in contrast with the interpretation of our own living body as a physical body like others, which would not be possible without empathy. <101>

Empathy proves to have yet another side as an aid to comprehending ourselves. As Scheler has shown us, inner perception contains within it the possibility of deception. Empathy now offers itself to us as a corrective for such deceptions along with further corroboratory or contradictory perceptual acts. It is possible for another to "judge me more accurately" than I judge myself and give me clarity about myself. For example, he notices that I look around me for approval as I show kindness, while I myself think I am acting out of pure generosity. This is how empathy and inner perception work hand in hand to give me myself to myself.

Chapter IV

Empathy as the Understanding of Spiritual Persons

1. The Concept of the Spirit and of the Cultural Sciences [Geisteswissenschaften]*

So far we have considered the individual "I" as a part of <101> nature, the living body as a physical body among others, the soul as founded on it, effects suffered and done and aligned in the causal order, all that is psychic as natural occurrence, consciousness as reality. Alone, this interpretation cannot be followed through consistently. In the constitution of the psycho-physical individual something already gleamed through in a number of places that goes beyond these frames. Consciousness appeared not only as a causally conditioned occurrence, but also as object-constituting at the same time. Thus it stepped out of the order of <102> nature and faced it. Consciousness as a correlate of the object world is not nature, but spirit.

We do not want to venture into the new problem arising here in its entirety, not to mention solving it. But neither can we avoid it if we want to take a position on questions confronting us in the history of the literature on empathy, questions concerning the understanding of foreign personalities. We shall see later how this is related.

*Please refer to the *Notes on the Translation*, p. xxv above.

91

First of all, we want to determine how far the spirit has already crept into our constitution of the psycho-physical individual. We have already taken along the "I" of the foreign living body as a spiritual subject by interpreting this body as the center of orientation of the spatial world, for we have thus ascribed to the foreign living body an object-constituting consciousness and considered the outer world as its correlate. All outer perception is carried out in spiritual acts. Similarly, in every literal act of empathy, i.e., in every comprehension of an act of feeling, we have already penetrated into the realm of the spirit. For, as physical nature is constituted in perceptual acts, so a new object realm is constituted in feeling. This is the world of values. In joy the subject has something joyous facing him, in fright something frightening, in fear something threatening. Even moods have their objective correlate. For him who is cheerful, the world is bathed in a rosy glow; for him who is depressed, bathed in black. And all this is co-given with acts of feeling as belonging to them. It is primarily appearances of expression that grant us access to these experiences. As we consider expressions to be proceeding from experiences, we have the spirit here simultaneously reaching into the physical world, the spirit "becoming visible" in the living body. This is made possible by the psychic reality of acts as experiences of a psycho-physical individual, and it involves an effect on physical nature.

This is revealed still more strikingly in the realm of the will. What is willed not only has an object correlate facing the volition, but, since volition releases action out of itself, it gives what is willed reality; volition becomes creative. Our whole "cultural world," all that "the hand of man" has formed, all utilitarian <103> objects, all works of handicraft, applied science, and art are the reality correlative to the spirit. Natural science (physics, chemistry, and biology in the broadest sense as the science of living nature, which also includes empirical psychology) describes natural objects and seeks to clarify their real genesis causally. The ontology of nature seeks to reveal the essence and the categorical structure of these objects.[115] And "natural philosophy" or (in order to avoid this disreputable word) the phenomenology of nature indicates how objects of this kind are constituted within consciousness. Thus it provides a clarifying elucidation of how these "dogmatic" sciences proceed. They themselves make no justification of their methods and should do so.

The *Geisteswissenschaften* [cultural sciences] describe the products of the spirit, though this alone does not satisfy them. They also pursue, mostly unseparated from this, what they call "history" in the broadest sense. This includes cultural history, literary history, history of language, art history, etc. They pursue the formation of spiritual products or their birth in the spirit. They do not go about this by causal explanation, but by a comprehension that relives history. (Were cultural scientists to proceed by causal explanation, they would be making use of the method of natural science. This is only permissible for elucidating the genetic process of cultural products insofar as it is a natural occurrence. Thus there is a physiology of language and a psychology of language, which, for example, investigate what organs have a part in making sounds and what psychic processes lead to the fact that one word is substituted for another with a similar sound. These investigations have their value, only one should not believe that these are true problems of philology or of the history of language.) As it pursues the formative process of spiritual products, we find the spirit itself to be at work. More exactly, a spiritual subject empathically seizes another and brings its operation to givenness to itself.

Only most recently has the clarification of the method of the cultural sciences been set about seriously. The great cultural scientists have indeed taken the right course (as some publications by Ranke and Jacob Burkhardt show) and also have been "very well aware of the right course," even if not with clear insight. But if it is possible to proceed correctly without insight into one's procedure, a misinterpretation of one's own problems must necessarily cause undesirable consequences in the functioning of the science itself. Earlier, people made unreasonable demands of natural science. It was to make natural occurrences "intelligible" (perhaps to prove that nature was a creation of the spirit of God). As long as natural science made no objections to this, it could not develop properly. Today there is the opposite danger. Elucidating causally is not enough, but people set up causal elucidation <104>

absolutely as the scientific ideal. This would be harmless if this interpretation were confined to natural scientists. One could calmly allow them the satisfaction of looking down on "unscientific" (because not "exact") cultural science, if the enthusiasm for this method had not gripped cultural scientists themselves. People do not want to be inexact and so cultural sciences have gone along in many ways and have lost sight of their own goals. We find the psychological interpretation of history[116] advocated in the textbooks on historical method. The study of this interpretation is emphatically recommended to young historians by Bernheim, for example, who ranks as an authority in the area of methodology.

We certainly do not maintain that psychological findings can be of no use at all to the historian. But they help him find out what is beyond his scope and do not yield him his real objectives. It is necessary for me to explain psychologically when I can no longer understand.[117] But when I do this, I am proceeding as a natural scientist and not as an historian. If I ascertain that an historical <105> personality showed certain psychic disturbances as the result of an illness, for example a loss of memory, I am establishing a natural event of the past. This is an historical occurrence as little as the eruption of Vesuvius that destroyed Pompeii. I can account for this natural event by laws (assuming that I have such laws), but it does not thus become in the least intelligible. The only thing that one is to "understand" is how such natural events motivate the conduct of these people. They have historical significance as "motives." But then one is no longer interpreting them as natural facts to be explained by natural laws. Should I "explain" the whole life of the past, I would have accomplished quite a piece of work in natural science, but would have completely destroyed the spirit of the past and gotten not one grain of historical knowledge. If historians take their task to be the determination and explanation of the psychological facts of the past, there is no longer any historical science.

Dilthey calls Taine's historical works a horrible example of the results of this psychological interpretation. Wilhelm Dilthey's goal in life was to give the cultural sciences their true foundation. He stressed that explanatory psychology was not capable of this and wanted to put a "descriptive and analytic psychology" in its place.[118] We believe that "descriptive" is not the proper word, for descriptive psychology is also the science of the soul as nature. Such a psychology can give us as little information on how the cultural sciences proceed as on the procedure of natural science. Phenomenology urges that reflecting investigation of this scientific consciousness make clear the method of cultural science as well as that of natural science. Dilthey is not completely clear here.

Indeed, he also sees "self consciousness" as the way to an epistemological grounding.[119] And he recognizes reflective turning of the glance toward the procedure of the cultural sciences to be the understanding that makes it possible for us to relive the spiritual life of the past.[120] (We would call this empathic comprehension.) But he finds man as nature or the total life of the psycho-physical individual to be the subject of this understand- <106> ing.[121] Therefore, the science occupied with human beings as nature, i.e., descriptive psychology, is the presupposition of the cultural sciences on the one hand, and on the other hand, what gives them unity; for cultural sciences are concerned with the single ramifications exemplifying this totality as a whole. These include art, morality, law, etc.

But now the principal difference between nature and spirit has been suspended. Exact natural science is also presented as a unity. Each one of these sciences has an abstract part of the concrete "natural object" for its object. The soul and the psycho-physical individual are also natural objects. Empathy was necessary for the constitution of these objects, and so to a certain extent our own individual was assumed. But spiritual understanding, which we shall characterize in still more detail, must be distinguished from this empathy.[122] But from Dilthey's mistaken expositions, we learn that there must be an objective basis for the cultural sciences beside the clarification of method, an ontology of the spirit corresponding to the ontology of nature. As natural things have an essential underlying structure, such as the fact that empirical spatial forms are realizations of ideal geometric forms, so there is also an essential structure of the spirit and of ideal types. Historical personalities are empirical realizations of these types. If empathy is the perceptual consciousness in which foreign persons come to givenness for us, then it is also the exemplary basis for obtaining this ideal type, just as natural perception is the basis for the eidetic knowledge of nature. We must therefore also find access to these problems from the point of view of our considerations.

2. The Spiritual Subject

<107>   Let us first establish what we have already obtained toward knowledge of the spiritual subject in constituting the psychophysical individual. We found the spiritual subject to be an "I" in whose acts an object world is constituted and which itself creates objects by reason of its will. If we consider the fact that not every subject sees the world from the same "side" or has it given in the same succession of appearances, but that everyone has his peculiar "Weltanschauung," we already have a characterization of the spiritual subject.

However, something in us opposes our recognition of what is commonly called a person in this "spiritual subject" so strikingly without substratum. Nevertheless, we can characterize it still further on the basis of our earlier expositions. Spiritual acts do not stand beside one another without relationship, like a cone of rays with the pure "I" as the point of intersection, but one act experientially proceeds from the other. The "I" passes over from one act to the other in the form of what we earlier called "motivation." This experiential "meaning context," so strangely excepted in the midst of psychic and psycho-physical causal relationships and without parallel in physical nature, is completely attributable to spirit. Motivation in the lawfulness of spiritual life. The experiential context of spiritual subjects is an experienced (primordially or empathically) totality of meaning and intelligible as such. Precisely this meaningful proceeding distinguishes motivation from psychic causality as well as empathic understanding of spiritual contexts from empathic comprehension of psychic contexts. A feeling by its meaning motivates an expression, and this meaning defines the limits of a range of possible expressions just as the meaning of a part of a sentence prescribes its possible formal and material complements. This asserts nothing more than that spiritual acts are subject to a general rational lawfulness. Thus, there are also rational laws for feeling, willing, and conduct <108> expressed in *a priori* sciences as well as laws for thinking. Axiology, ethics, and practice take their places beside logic.

This rational lawfulness is distinguishable from essential lawfulness. Willing is essentially motivated by a feeling. Therefore, an unmotivated willing is an impossibility. There is no conceivable subject with a nature to want something which does not appear to it as valuable. Willing by its meaning (that posits something to be realized) is directed toward what is possible, i.e., realizable. Rationally, one can only will the possible. But there are irrational people who do not care whether what they have recognized as valuable is realizable or not. They will it for its value alone, attempting to make the impossible possible. Pathological psychic life indicates that what is contradictory to rational laws is really possible for many people. We call this mental derangement. Moreover, psychic lawfulness can here be completely intact. On the other hand, in some psychic illnesses rational laws of the spirit remain completely intact, for example, in anesthesia, aphasia, etc. We recognize a radical difference between spiritual and psychic anomalies. In cases of the second kind, the intelligibility of foreign psychic life is completely undisturbed; we must only empathize changed causal relationships. However, in mental illness we can no longer understand because we can only empathize a causal sequence separately and not a meaningful proceeding of experiences.

Finally, there is still a series of pathological cases in which neither the psychic mechanism nor rational lawfulness seems to be severed. Rather, these cases are experiential modifications of the frame of rational laws, for example, depression following a catastrophic event. Not only is the portion of the psychic life spared by the illness intelligible here, but also the pathological symptom itself.[123] These considerations lead us to the conclusion that the spiritual subject is essentially subject to rational laws and that its experiences are intelligibly related.   <109>

Edith Stein

3. The Constitution of the Person in Emotional Experiences

But even this does not satisfy us. Even now, we have not yet reached what is called a person. Rather, it is worth looking into the fact that something else is constituted in spiritual acts besides the object world so far considered. It is an old psychological tradition that the "I" is constituted in emotions.[124] We want to see what can be meant by this "I" and whether we can demonstrate this contention.

Traditionally, psychologists distinguish sensations in which I sense "something," an interpretation with which we do not completely agree, from emotions in which I feel "myself" or acts and states of the "I." What kind of meaning can this distinction have? We have seen that all acts are "I" experiences in each one of which we run into the "I" as we reflect. Further, feeling is also the feeling of something, a giving act. On the other hand, every act must also be looked at as a state of the psychic "I" once this has been constituted.

However, there is a deeply penetrating difference in the sphere of experience. In "theoretical acts," such as acts of perception, imagination, relating or deductive thinking, etc., I am turned to an object in such a way that the "I" and the acts are not there at all. There is always the possibility of throwing a reflecting glance on these, since they are always accomplished and ready for perception. But it is equally possible for this not to happen, for the "I" to be entirely absorbed in considering the object. It is possible to conceive of a subject only living in theoretical acts having an object world facing it without ever becoming aware of itself and

<110> its consciousness, without "being there" for itself. But this is no longer possible as soon as this subject not only perceives, thinks, etc., but also feels. For as it feels it not only experiences objects, but it itself. It experiences emotions as coming from the "depth of its 'I'." This also means that this "self"-experiencing "I" is not the pure "I," for the pure "I" has no depth. But the "I" experienced in emotion has levels of various depths. These are revealed as emotions arise out of them.

People want to distinguish between "feeling" [*Fühlen*] and "the feeling" [*Gefühl*]. I do not believe that these two designations indicate different kinds of experiences, but only different "directions" of the same experience. Feeling is an experience when it gives us an object or else something about an object. The feeling is the same act when it appears to be originating out of the "I" or unveiling a level of the "I." Yet we still need a particular turning of the glance to make the feelings as they burst out of the "I," and this "I" itself in a pregnant sense, into an object. We need a turning specifically different from reflection because reflection does not show me something not previously there for me at all. On the other hand, this turning is specifically different from the transition from a "background experience," the act in which an object faces me but is not the object toward which I prefer to turn as the specific cogito, the act in which I am directed toward the object in the true sense. For turning to the feeling, etc., is not a transition from one object givenness to another, but the objectifying of something subjective.[125] Further, in feelings we experience ourselves not only as present, but also as constituted in such and such a way. They announce personal attributes to us. We have already spoken of persistent attributes of the soul announced in experiences. We gave examples of such persistent attributes, among others, memory announced in our recollections and passion revealed in our emotions.

A closer consideration shows this summary to be most superfi-   <111> cial, since it is in no way dealing with comparable attributes. They are ontological (in regard to their position in the essential structure of the soul) as well as phenomenological (in regard to their constitution in terms of consciousness). We would never arrive at something like "memory" by living in recollection and turning to the recollected object. Also memory is first given to us in inner perception. These are new acts in which the recollection not present for us before is "given," and these acts announce the soul and its attribute (or "capacity" [*Fähigkeit*]). In "overwhelming joy" or "upsetting pain" I become aware of my suffering and the place it occupies in the "I." This occurs as I undergo the suffering itself without its having been "given" in new acts. I do not perceive it, but experience it.

On the contrary, we can just as easily objectify these experienced attributes as we can the feelings. For example, such an objectification is necessarily forthcoming if we want to say something about the attributes. These objectifying acts are, again, giving acts (considering them as acts of perceiving or as merely indicating) and in them there arises the complete coincidence of the experienced and the perceived "I."

In order to arrive at a complete picture, we would have to go through every kind of experience. This can take place only suggestively here. Sensations result in nothing for the experienced "I." The pressure, warmth, or attraction to light that I sense are nothing in which I experience myself, in no way issue from my "I." On the contrary, if they are made into an object, they "announce" "sensitivity" to me as a persistent psychic attribute. The so-called "sensations of feeling" or "sensory feelings," such as pleasure in a tactile impression or sensory pain, already reach into the sphere of the "I." I experience pleasure and pain on the surface of my "I." At the same time I also experience my "sensory receptiveness" as the topmost or outermost layer of my "I." [126]

<112> There are, then, feelings which are "self-experiencing" in a special sense: general feelings and moods. I distinguish general feelings from moods because general feelings "are bound to the living body," which should not be drawn in here. General feelings and moods occupy a special place in the realm of consciousness, for they are not giving acts but only visible as "colorings" of giving acts. Therefore, at the same time they are different because they have no definite locality in the "I," are neither experienced on the surface of the "I" nor in its depths and expose no levels of the "I." Rather, they inundate and fill it entirely. They penetrate, or certainly can penetrate, all levels. They have something of the omnipresence of light. For example, cheerfulness of character is not an experienced attribute, either, that is localized in the "I" in any way but is poured over it entirely like a bright luster. And every actual experience has in it something of this "total illumination," is bathed in it.

Now we come to feelings in the pregnant sense. As said earlier, these feelings are always feelings of something. Every time I feel, I am turned toward an object, something of an object is given to me, and I see a level of the object. But, in order to see a level of the object, I must first have it. It must be given to me in theoretical acts. Thus, the structure of all feelings requires theoretical acts. When I am joyful over a good deed, this is how the deed's goodness or its positive value faces me. But I must know about the deed in order to be joyful over it—knowledge is fundamental to joy. An intuitive perceptual or conceptual comprehension can also be substituted for this knowledge underlying the feeling of value. Furthermore, this knowledge belongs among acts that can only be comprehended reflectively and has no "I" depth of any kind.

On the contrary, the feeling based on this knowledge always reaches into the "I's" stability and is experienced as issuing out of <113> it. And this even takes place during complete immersion in felt value. Anger over the loss of a piece of jewelry comes from a more superficial level or does not penetrate as deeply as losing the same object as the souvenir of a loved one. Furthermore, pain over the loss of this person himself would be even deeper. This discloses essential relationships among the hierarchy of felt values,[127] the depth classification of value feelings, and the level classification of the person exposed in these feelings. Accordingly, every time we advance in the value realm, we also make acquisitions in the realm of our own personality. This correlation makes feelings and their firm establishment in the "I" rationally lawful as well as making possible decisions about "right" and "wrong" in this domain. If someone is "overcome" by the loss of his wealth (i.e., if it gets him at the kernel point of his "I"), he feels "irrational." He inverts the value hierarchy or loses sensitive insight into higher values altogether, causing him to lack the correlative personal levels.

Sentiments of love and hate, thankfulness, vengeance, animosity, etc.—feelings with other people for their object—are also sensitive acts exposing personal levels. These feelings, too, are firmly established in various levels of the "I." For example, love is deeper than inclination. On the other hand, their correlate is other people's values. If these values are not derived values that belong to the person like other realized or comprehended values, but his own values, if they come to givenness in acts rooted in another depth than the feeling of non-personal values, if, accordingly, they unveil levels not to be experienced in any way, then the comprehension of foreign persons is constitutive of our own person. Now, in the act of love we have a comprehending or an intending of the value of a person. This is not a valuing for any other sake. We do not love a person because he does good. His <114> value is not that he does good, even if he perhaps comes to light for this reason. Rather, he himself is valuable and we love him "for his own sake." And the ability to love, evident in our loving, is rooted in another depth from the ability to value morally, experienced in the values of deeds. There are essential relationships among the value feeling and the feeling of the value of its reality (for the reality of a value is itself a value), and its "I" depth. The depth of a feeling of value determines the depth of a feeling based on the comprehension of the existence of this value. This second feeling, however, is not of the same depth. Pain over the loss of a loved one is not as deep as the love for this person, if the loss means that this person ceases to exist. As the personal value outlasts his existence and the love outlasts the joy over the loved one's existence, so the personal value is also higher than the value of his reality, and this former feeling of value is more deeply rooted.[128] But should "loss of the person" mean suspending the person and his value so that possibly this empirical person continues to exist, such as in a case where "one has been deceived by a person," then pain over the loss is synonymous with suspension of love and is rooted in the same depth.

The comprehension of values is itself a positive value. But to become aware of this value, one must be directed toward this comprehension. In turning to the value, the feeling of value is certainly there, but it is not an object. For its value to be felt, it must first be made into an object. In such a feeling of value of the feeling of value (joy over my joy) I become aware of myself in a double manner as subject and as object. Again, the original and the reflected feeling of value will take hold in different depths. Thus I can enjoy a work of art and at the same time enjoy my enjoyment of it. The enjoyment of the work of art will "reasonably" be the deeper one. We call the "inversion" of this relationship "perversion." This does not mean that the unreflected feeling must always be the deeper one. I can feel a slight malicious joy <115> at another's misfortune and can suffer deeply in this slight malicious joy. This is rightly so. Depth classification does not directly depend on the antithesis of reflected—non-reflected, but, again, on the hierarchy of felt values. To value a positive value positively is less valuable than the positive value itself. To value a negative value positively is less valuable than the negative value itself. To prefer the positive valuing over the positive value is thus axiologically unreasonable. To put the unjustified positive value behind the negative one is axiologically reasonable.

According to this, the value of our own person seems to be only reflexive and not constituted in the immediate directedness of experience. We need yet another investigation to decide this. Not only comprehending, but also realizing, a value is a value. We want to consider this realizing in more detail, not as willing and acting, but only its emotional components. In realizing a value, this value to be realized is before me, and this feeling of value plays the role in constituting personality that we have already attributed to it. But, simultaneously with this feeling of value, there is an entirely naive and unreflected joy in "creation." In this joy the creation is felt to be a value. At the same time I experience my creative strength in this creation and myself as the person who is provided with this strength. I experience creativity as valuable in itself. The strength I experience in creation and its simultaneous power, or the very power of being able to create itself, are autonomous personal values and, above all, entirely independent of the value to be realized.

The naive "feeling of self value" of this creative strength is further shown in realizing, and in the experience of being able to realize, a negative value. Then, to be sure, values compete; and the positive value of my own strength can be absorbed in the negative average value of it. Nevertheless, we have an example here of unreflected "self emotions" in which the person experiences himself as valuable.

Before we go over into the domain of experiences of the will, whose threshold we have already stood upon, we must pursue still another "dimension" of the significance of feelings for the con- <116> stitution of personality. They not only have the peculiarity of being rooted in a certain depth of the "I" but also of filling it out to more or less of an extent. Moods have already shown us what this means. We can say that every feeling has a certain mood component that causes the feeling to be spread throughout the "I" from the feeling's place of origin and fill it up. Starting from a peripheral level, a slight resentment can fill me "entirely," but it can also happen upon a deep joy that prevents it from pushing further forward to the center. Now, in turn, this joy progresses victoriously from the center to the periphery and fills out all the layers above it. In terms of our previous metaphor, feelings are like different sources of light on whose position and luminosity the resulting illumination depends.

The metaphor of light and color can illustrate the relationship between feelings and moods for us in still another respect. Emotions can have mood components essentially and occasionally just as colors have a specific brightness over and above their higher or lower degrees of brightness. So there is a serious and a cheerful joy. Apart from this, however, joy has specifically a "luminous" character.

On the other hand, we can still further elucidate the nature of moods from these relationships between moods and feelings. I can not only experience a mood and myself in it, but also its penetration into me. For example, I can experience it as resulting from a specific experience. I experience how "something" upsets me. This "something" is always the correlate of an act of feeling, such as the absence of news over which I am angry, the scratching violin that offends me, the raw deal over which I am irritated. The "reach" of the aroused mood, then, depends on the "I" depth of the act of feeling correlative with the height of the felt value. The level to which I can "reasonably" allow it to penetrate is prescribed.

<117> Along with depth and reach of the feelings, a third dimension is their duration. They not only fill up the "I" in its depth and width, but also in the "length" of experienced time they remain in it. And here there is also a specific duration of the feeling dependent on depth. How long a feeling or a mood "may remain" in me, filling me out or ruling me, is also subject to rational laws. This dependence of the person's structure on rational laws, now already variously demonstrated, is clearly distinguished from the soul's subordination, not to reason, but to natural laws.

We must distinguish their intensity from the depth, reach, and duration of feelings. A slight moodiness can hang on for a long time and can fill me out to more or less of a degree. Further, I can feel a high value less intensive than a lower one and thus be induced to realize the lower instead of the higher one. "Induced!" Here lies the fact that rational lawfulness has been infringed upon. The stronger feeling properly has the greater value and so this also sets the will in motion. But it is not always actually so. For example, we have already often noted that the least mishap in our environment tends to excite us much more strongly than a catastrophe in another part of the world without our mistaking which event is more significant. Is this because we do not have the intuitional foundations for a primordial valuing in the one case, or is contagion of feeling operative in the other? Anyway, we seem to be dealing here with an effect of psycho-physical organization.

We have discerned that every feeling has a specific intensity. Now we must still comprehend how the stronger feeling guides the will. However, we cannot understand the feeling's actual strength any further, but can only explain it causally. Perhaps one could show that every individual has a total measure of psychic strength determining intensity, which intensity may claim every single experience. So the rational duration of a feeling can exceed an individual's "psychic strength." Then it will either expire prematurely or bring about a "psychic collapse." (One would call the first case a "normal" turn, the second case an "abnormal" or <118> pathological turn. The "norm" under discussion here is that used by biologists, not a rational one. Not the feeling, but succumbing to it, is pathological.) Nevertheless, this is not the place to go into this question more deeply.

We must still settle the analysis of experiences of will. We must also investigate the strivings related to them in their possible significance for the constitution of personality. According to Pfänder, strivings seem to have such a significance. He says:

> Strivings and counter-strivings existing in the "I" do
> not really have the same position in this "I." Namely,
> this "I" has an individual structure: The true "I"

center or the "I" kernel is surrounded by the "I"
body. Now, strivings can indeed exist in the "I" but
outside of the "I" center in the "I" body. Thus in
this sense they can be experienced as eccentric
strivings.[129]

The distinction between "I" kernel and "I" body seems to be in
accordance with our distinction between central and peripheral
personal levels. Therefore, central and eccentric strivings would
burst forth from different levels, have different "I" depths. However, this description does not seem to me correct. The really
justified distinction between central and eccentric strivings seems
to be entirely different. As far as I can see, we are talking about
different modalities of accomplishing the act of striving. Central
striving is a striving in the form of the cogito; eccentric strivings
are the corresponding "background experiences." But this does
not mean that striving has no "I" depth at all. If a noise arouses in
me the striving to turn myself toward it, unless I reflect I do not
actually find that I experience something here other than the
pure "I" on which the "pull" is exercised. Nor do I experience it
as arising out of some depth or other. On the contrary, sometimes
I experience "sources" from which the striving proceeds,[130] such
as a discomfort, a restlessness, or something similar. Because they
originate in this source, strivings have a secondary depth and
<119> constitutive significance for personality, namely, if personality's
source first becomes visible in striving. Furthermore, the stubbornness and the intensity of a striving then turns out to be
dependent on the "I" depth of its source and thus accessible to a
rational lawfulness. Meanwhile, the pure striving that does not
arise experientially out of a feeling is neither rational nor irrational.

According to Pfänder, willing is always "I" centered in contrast
with striving.[131] We agree with him when we translate this into
our interpretation. The volitional decision is always carried out in
the form of the "cogito." As we already know, this says nothing
about the will as "self experiencing." According to Pfänder:

If it is to be a genuine volition, then our own "I"
must not only be thought but be immediately com-

prehended itself and be made into an objective subject of the practical intentions. Thus volition, but not
striving, is immediately self-conscious. Volition is
thus a practical act of determination impregnated by
a definite intention of the will. It goes out of the "I"
center and, pressing forward to the "I" itself, de-
cides the definite future behavior of this self. It is an
act of self determination in the sense that the "I" is
the subject as well as the object of the act.

We do not completely agree with this analysis, either. The
object of volition is what is willed or what the will posits. In
experiential terms, a self determination of a future attitude is
only present in the willing of a future act, not in the simple willing
of an attitude to be realized. Thus, in simple willing the "I" is not
an object. On the contrary, it is always experienced on the subject
side as follows: "I" shall give being to what is not. At first this is
only the pure "I." But because every willing is based on a feeling
and, further, this feeling of "being able to be realized" is linked
with every willing, every willing invades the personal structure in
a double manner and exposes its depths. Thus, in every free,
indubitable "I will" lies an "I can." Only a shy "I would like" is in
harmony with an "I cannot." "I will, but I cannot," is nonsense. <120>

We must examine the position of theoretical acts still further.
First of all, they seem to us to be entirely irrelevant to personality's structure, not at all rooted in it. Yet we have already encoun-
tered them a number of times and can presume that they must be
involved in various ways. Every act of feeling as well as every act
of willing is based on a theoretical act. Thus a purely feeling
subject is an impossibility. Nevertheless, from this side theoretical
acts only appear as conditions and not as constituents of personality. Nor do I believe that simple acts of perception have a greater
significance. It is different with definite cognitive acts. Knowledge is itself a value and indeed a value always graduated according to its object. The act of reflection in which knowledge comes
to givenness can thus always become a basis for a valuing; and
knowledge, like every felt value, therefore becomes relevant for
personality's structure.

Yet this range of values is not merely accessible to the reflecting glance. Not only the knowledge we have but, perhaps to a still greater extent, the knowledge not yet realized is felt as a value. This feeling of value is the source of all cognitive striving and "what is at the bottom" of all cognitive willing. An object proffers itself to me as dark, veiled, and unclear. It stands there as something which demands exposure and clarification. The clarifying and unveiling with their result in clear and plain knowledge stand before me as a penetratingly felt value and drag me irresistibly into them. A range of my own values is made accessible here, and a level of my own personality corresponds to it. This is a very deep level repeatedly passing for the kernel level as such. It really is the essential kernel of a certain personal type of a definitely "scientific nature."

But we can take still more from the analysis of knowledge. We spoke of cognitive striving and cognitive willing. The cognitive <121> process itself is an activity, a deed. I not only feel the value of the cognition to be realized and joy in the realized one, but in the realizing itself I also feel that strength and power we found in other willing and action.

Thus we have sketched the constitution of personality in outline. We have found it to be a unity entirely based in experience and further distinguished by its subordination to rational laws. Person and world (more exactly, value world) were found to be completely correlated. An indication of this correlation is sufficient for our purposes. Hence, it follows that it is impossible to formulate a doctrine of the person (for which we naturally take no responsibility here) without a value doctrine, and that the person can be obtained from such a value doctrine. The ideal person with all his values in a suitable hierarchy and having adequate feelings would correspond to the entire realm of value levels. Other personal types would result from the abolition of certain value ranges or from the modification of the value hierarchy and, further, from differences in the intensity of value experiences or from preferring one of the several forms of expression, such as bodily expression, willing, action, etc. Perhaps the formulation of a doctrine of types would provide the ontological foundation of the cultural sciences intended by Dilthey's efforts.

4. The Givenness of the Foreign Person

Now we still must determine how the foreign person's constitution is in contrast with our own and, furthermore, how the person is distinguished from the psycho-physical individual with whose constitution we were occupied earlier. After all the previous investigations, the first task no longer seems to offer any great difficulties. As my own person is constituted in primordial spiritual acts, so the foreign person is constituted in empathically experienced acts. I experience his every action as proceeding from a will and this, in turn, from a feeling. Simultaneously with this, I am given a level of his person and a range of values in principle experienceable by him. This, in turn, meaningfully motivates the expectation of future possible volitions and actions. Accordingly, a single action and also a single bodily expression, such as a look or a laugh, can give me a glimpse into the kernel of   <122> the person. Further questions arising here can be answered when we have discussed the relationship between "soul" and "person."

5. Soul and Person

We saw persistent attributes in both the soul and the person. But qualities of the soul are constituted for inner perception and for empathy when they make experiences into objects. By contrast, persons are revealed in original experiencing or in empathic projection. This is so even if we still need a special turning of the glance in order to make the "awareness" into a comprehension, as in these experiences themselves. There are characteristics (or "dispositions") only in principle perceivable and not experienceable. This is true of the memory announced for the comprehending glance in my recollections. These are thus psychic in a specific sense. Naturally, personal attributes, such as goodness, readiness to make sacrifices, the energy I experience in my activities, also become psychic when they are perceived in a psycho-physical individual. But they are also conceivable as attributes of a purely spiritual subject and continue to retain their own nature in the context of psycho-physical organization. They reveal their special position by standing outside of the causal order. We found the soul with its experiences and all its characteristics to be dependent on all kinds of circumstances that could be influenced by one another as well as by the states and the character of the living body. Finally, we found it incorporated into the whole order of physical and psychic reality. The individual with all his characteristics develops under the constant impression of such influences so that this person has such a nature because he was exposed to such and such influences. Under other circumstances he would have developed differently. There is something empirically fortuitous in this "nature." One can conceive of it as modified in many ways. But this variability is not unlimited; there are limits here.

<123>

We find not only that the categorical structure of the soul as soul must be retained, but also within its individual form we strike an unchangeable kernel, the personal structure. I can think of Caesar in a village instead of in Rome and can think of him transferred into the twentieth century. Certainly, his historically settled individuality would then go through some changes, but just as surely he would remain Caesar. The personal structure marks off a range of possibilities of variation within which the person's real distinctiveness can be developed "ever according to circumstances." As we said earlier, capacities of the soul can be cultivated by use and can also be dulled. I can be "trained" by practice to enjoy works of art, and the enjoyment can also be ruined by frequent repetition. But only because of my psychophysical organization am I subject to the "power of habit." A purely spiritual subject feels a value and experiences the correlative level of its nature in it. This emotion can become neither deeper nor less deep. A value inaccessible to it remains so. A spiritual subject does not lose a value it feels. Neither can a psycho-physical individual be led by habit to a value for which he lacks the correlative level. The levels of the person do not "develop" or "deteriorate," but they can only be exposed or not in the course of psychic development.

This goes for "intersubjective" as well as for "intrasubjective" causality. The person as such is not subject to the contagion of feeling. Rather, this veils the true content of personality. The life circumstances in which an individual grows up can breed in him a distaste for certain actions not conforming to any original personal attribute, so that it can be removed by other "influences." An instance is authoritative moral education. If he who has been educated in "moral principles" and who behaves according to them looks "into himself," he will perceive with satisfaction a "virtuous" man. This is true until one day, in an action bursting forth from deep inside of him, he experiences himself as someone of an entirely different nature from the person he thought him- <124> self to be until then. One can only speak of a person developing under the influence of the circumstances of life or of a "signifi- cance of the milieu for the character," as Dilthey also says,[132] insofar as the real environment is the object of his value experi- encing and determines which levels are exposed and which possi- ble actions become actual.

So the psycho-physical empirical person can be a more or less complete realization of the spiritual one. It is conceivable for a man's life to be a complete process of his personality's unfolding; but it is also possible that psycho-physical development does not permit a complete unfolding, and, in fact, in different ways. He who dies in childhood or falls victim of a paralysis cannot unfold "himself" completely. An empirical contingency, the weakness of the organism, destroys the meaning of life (if we see the meaning of life to be this unfolding of the person). On the other hand, a stronger organism continues to support life when its meaning is already fulfilled and the person has completely developed him- self. The incompleteness is here similar to the fragmentary char- acter of a work of art of which a part is finished and only the raw material for the rest is preserved. A defective unfolding is also possible in a sound organism. He who never meets a person worthy of love or hate can never experience the depths in which love and hate are rooted. To him who has never seen a work of art nor gone beyond the walls of the city may perhaps forever be closed the enjoyment of nature and art together with his suscep- tibility for this enjoyment. Such an "incomplete" person is similar to an unfinished sketch. Finally, it is also conceivable for the personality not to unfold at all. He who does not feel values himself but acquires all feelings only through contagion from others, cannot experience "himself." He can become, not a personality, but at most a phantom of one.

<125>   Only in the last case can we say that there is no spiritual person present. In all other cases we must not put the person's non-unfolding on a par with his non-existence. Rather, the spiritual person also exists even if he is not unfolded. As the realization of the spiritual person, the psycho-physical individual can be called the "empirical person." As "nature" he is subject to the laws of causality, as "spirit" to the laws of meaning. Also that meaningful context of psychic attributes of which we spoke earlier, by virtue of which the comprehension of one attribute reasonably motivates progress to the other, is his only as a personal one. Finest sensitivity to ethical values and a will leaving them completely unheeded and only allowing itself to be guided by sensual motives do not go together in the unity of a meaning, are unintelligible. And so an action also bids for understanding. It is not merely to be carried out empathically as a single experience, but experienced as proceeding meaningfully from the total structure of the person.[133]

6. The Existence of the Spirit

Simmel has said that the intelligibility of characters vouches for their objectivity, that it constitutes "historical truth." To be sure, he does not distinguish this truth from poetic truth. A creature of the free imagination can also be an intelligible person. Moreover, historical objects must be real. Some kind of point of departure, such as a trait of the historical character, must be given to me in order to demonstrate the meaning context the object reveals to me as an historical fact. But if I get possession of it, in whatever manner, I have an existing product and not a merely fantasized one. In empathic comprehension of the foreign spiritual individual, I also have the possibility of bringing his unverified behavior to givenness under certain circumstances. Such action is demanded by his personal structure of which I know. If he should actually act differently, disturbing influences of psycho-physical
<126>   organization have hindered his person from being freely lived out.

But since such disturbing influences are possible, this statement has the character of an assertion about empirical existence

[*Dasein*], and I may not deliver it as a factual statement. But the mere factual statement alone is even less "true historically." The most exact statement of all that Frederick the Great did from the day of his birth up to his last breath does not give us a glimmer of the spirit which, transforming, reached into the history of Europe. Yet the understanding glance may seize upon this in a chance remark in a short letter. The mere concatenation of facts makes a meaningful occurrence into a blind occurrence causally ruled. It neglects the world of the spirit that is no less real or knowable than the natural world. Because man belongs to both realms, the history of mankind must take both into consideration. It should understand the forms of the spirit and of spiritual life and ascertain how much has become reality. And it can call on natural science to help explain what did not happen and what happened differently than the laws of the spirit demanded.[134]

7. Discussion in Terms of Dilthey

(a) The Being and Value of the Person

We have already stressed how much our interpretation is like Dilthey's. Even though he has not made the distinction in principle between nature and spirit, he also recognizes the rational lawfulness of spiritual life. He expresses it by saying that being and ought, fact and norm, are inseparably linked together in the cultural sciences.[135] The relationships of life are unities of value bearing the standard of their estimation in themselves. But we must still distinguish between rational lawfulness and value. Spiritual acts are experientially bound into contexts of a definite general form. People can bring these forms to givenness to themselves by a reflective standpoint and utter them in theoretical propositions. Such propositions can also be turned into equivalent propositions of ought. Thanks to this formal lawfulness, spiritual acts are subject to the estimation of "true" or "false." For example, there is the experienced unity of an action when a valuing motivates a volition. This is converted into practice as soon as the possibility of realization is given. Formulated as a theoretical proposition, we have here the general rational law: He

<127>

who feels a value and can realize it, does so. In normative terms: If you feel a value and can realize it, then do it.[136] Every action conforming to this law is rational or right. However, this determines nothing about the material value of the action; we only have the formal conditions of a valuable action. Rational laws have nothing to say about the action's material value. This makes the intelligible structures of experience into objects of a possible valuing, too, but these have not so far been constituted in empathic comprehension as value objects (except for the particular class of unreflected experiences of our own value which we noted).[137]

(b) Personal Types and the Conditions of the Possibility of Empathy With Persons

As we saw, Dilthey further contends that personalities have an experiential structure of a typical character. We also agree with him in this. Because of the correlation among values, the experiencing of value, and the levels of the person, all possible types of persons can be established a priori from the standpoint of a universal recognition of worth. Empirical persons are realizations of these types. On the other hand, every empathic comprehension of a personality means the acquisition of such a type.[138]

<128>

Now, in Dilthey and others we find the view that the intelligibility of foreign individuality is bound to our own individuality, that our experiential structure limits the range of what is for us intelligible. On a higher level, this is the repetition of possible empathic deception that we have shown in the constitution of the psychophysical individual. However, we have not demonstrated that this belongs to the essence of empathy or said that the individual character is made the basis for experiencing other individuals. Of course, in the case of the psycho-physical individual, we could assert that the typical character was the basis for "analogizing" rather than the individual one. What can we do about this here where every single person is already himself a type?

Now, types have various levels of generality in the realm of the spirit just as in the natural realm. In nature the most general type, the "living organism," marked off the range of empathic possibilities. The deeper we descended, the greater became the number of typical phenomena organisms had in common. It is not much different here. The individual experiential structure is an "eidetic singularity," the lowest differentiation of superimposed general types. Age, sex, occupation, station, nationality, generation are the kind of general experiential structures to which the individual is subordinate. So, among other things, the Gretchen type represents the type of the German country girl of the sixteenth century, i.e., the individual type is constituted through its "participation" in the more general one. And the topmost type marking off the range of the intelligible is that of the spiritual person or the value experiencing subject in general.

I consider every subject whom I empathically comprehend as experiencing a value as a person whose experiences interlock themselves into an intelligible, meaningful whole. How much of his experiential structure I can bring to my fulfilling intuition depends on my own structure. In principle, all foreign experience permitting itself to be derived from my own personal structure   <129> can be fulfilled, even if this structure has not yet actually unfolded. I can experience values empathically and discover correlative levels of my person, even though my primordial experience has not yet presented an opportunity for their exposure. He who has never looked a danger in the face himself can still experience himself as brave or cowardly in the empathic representation of another's situation.

By contrast, I cannot fulfill what conflicts with my own experiential structure. But I can still have it given in the manner of empty presentation. I can be skeptical myself and still understand that another sacrifices all his earthly goods to his faith. I see him behave in this way and empathize a value experiencing as the motive for his conduct. The correlate of this is not accessible to me, causing me to ascribe to him a personal level I do not myself possess. In this way I empathically gain the type of *homo religiosus* by nature foreign to me, and I understand it even though what newly confronts me here will always remain unfulfilled. Again, suppose others regulate their lives entirely by the acquisition of material goods, allowing everything else to take second place, which I consider unimportant. Then I see that higher ranges of value that I glimpse are closed to them; and I also understand these people, even though they are of a different type.

Now we see what justification Dilthey has for saying, "The interpretive faculty operating in the cultural sciences is the whole person." Only he who experiences himself as a person, as a meaningful whole, can understand other persons. And we also see why Ranke would have liked to "erase" his self in order to see things "as they were." The "self" is the individual experiential structure. The great master of those who know recognizes in it the source of deception from which danger threatens us. If we take the self as the standard, we lock ourselves into the prison of our <130> individuality. Others become riddles for us, or still worse, we remodel them into our image and so falsify historical truth.[139]

8. The Significance of Empathy for the Constitution of Our Own Person

We also see the significance of knowledge of foreign personality for "knowledge of self" in what has been said. We not only learn to make us ourselves into objects, as earlier, but through empathy with "related natures," i.e., persons of our type, what is "sleeping" in us is developed. By empathy with differently composed personal structures we become clear on what we are not, what we are more or less than others. Thus, together with self knowledge, we also have an important aid to self evaluation. Since the experience of value is basic to our own value, at the same time as new values are acquired by empathy, our own unfamiliar values become visible. When we empathically run into ranges of value closed to us, we become conscious of our own deficiency or disvalue. Every comprehension of different persons can become the basis of an understanding of value. Since, in the act of preference or disregard, values often come to givenness that remain unnoticed in themselves, we learn to assess ourselves correctly now and then. We learn to see that we experience ourselves as having more or less value in comparison with others.

9. The Question of the Spirit Being Based on the Physical Body

We have one more important question yet to discuss. We came to the spiritual person through the psycho-physical individual. In constituting the individual, we ran into the spirit. We moved freely in the context of spiritual life without recourse to corpore- <131> ality. Once having penetrated into this labyrinth, we found our way by the guideline of "meaning," but we have so far not found any other entrance than the one we used, the sensually perceivable expression in countenances, etc. or in actions.

Is it essentially necessary that spirit can only enter into exchange with spirit through the medium of corporeality? I, as psycho-physical individual, actually obtain information about the spiritual life of other individuals in no other way. Of course, I know of many individuals, living and dead, whom I have never seen. But I know this from others whom I see or through the medium of their works which I sensually perceive and which they have produced by virtue of their psycho-physical organization. We meet the spirit of the past in various forms but always bound to a physical body. This is the written or printed word or the word hewed into stone—the spatial form become stone or metal. But does not live communion unite me with contemporary spirits and tradition unite me immediately with spirits of the past without bodily mediation? Certainly I feel myself to be one with others and allow their emotions to become motives for my willing. However, this does not give me the others, but already presupposes their givenness. (And I consider as my own that which penetrates into me from others, living or dead, without my knowing it. This establishes no exchange of spirits.)

But now how is it with purely spiritual persons the idea of whom certainly contains no contradiction in itself? Is no exchange between them conceivable? There have been people who thought that in a sudden change of their person they experienced the effect of the grace of God, others who felt themselves to be guided in their conduct by a protective spirit. (We do not have to think just of Socrates' δαιμόνιον, which certainly should not be taken so literally.) Who can say whether there is genuine experience present here or whether there is that unclearness about our own motives which we found in considering the "idols of self knowledge"? But is not the essential possibility of genuine experi-

<132> ence in this area already given with the delusions of such experience? Nevertheless, the study of religious consciousness seems to me to be the most appropriate means of answering our question, just as, on the other hand, its answer is of most interest for the domain of religion. However, I leave the answering of this question to further investigation and satisfy myself here with a "non liquet," "It is not clear."

Personal Biography

I, Edith Stein, was born on October 12, 1891 in Breslau, the daughter of the deceased merchant Siegfried Stein and his wife Auguste, née Courant. I am a Prussian citizen and Jewish. From October 1897 to Easter 1906 I went to the Viktoriaschule (municipal lyceum) in Breslau, and from Easter 1908 to Easter 1911 to the Breslau Girls' Secondary School [*Studienanstalt realgymnasialer Richtung*] affiliated with it. Here I passed my school certificate examination. In October 1915 I obtained the leaving certificate of a humanistic gymnasium by taking a supplementary examination in Greek at Johannes Gymnasium in Breslau.

From Easter 1911 to Easter 1913 I studied philosophy, psychology, history and German philology at the University of Breslau, then for four more semesters at the University of Göttingen. In January 1915 I passed the *Staatsexamen pro facultate docendi* in philosophical propaedeutics, history, and German. At the end of this semester, I interrupted my studies and was for a time engaged in the service of the Red Cross. From February to October 1916 I replaced an indisposed secondary school teacher at the above mentioned Girls' Secondary School in Breslau. Then I moved to Freiburg in Br. in order to work as Professor Husserl's assistant.

At this time I would to extend my sincere thanks to all those who have offered me stimulation and challenge during my student days, but above all, to those of my teachers and student associates through whom an approach to phenomenological philosophy was opened to me: to Professor Husserl, Dr. Reinach, and the Göttingen Philosophical Society.

Notes

1. English translation: *Phenomenology of Perception*, trans. by Colin Smith (New York: The Humanities Press, 1962).
2. English translation: *The Nature of Sympathy*, trans. by Peter Heath (London: Routledge and Kegan Paul, 1954).
3. Edmund Husserl, *Ideas: General Introduction to Pure Phenomenology*, trans. by W. R. Boyce Gibson (second edition; New York: The Macmillan Company, 1952). References in brackets are to the sections in this edition to which E. Stein seems to be referring.
4. Cf. *Ideas, op. cit.*, Section 60.
5. Cf. p. 23 of the original; p. 22 this ed.
6. Cf. p. 10 of the original; p. 11 this ed.
7. cf. p. 10 of the original; p. 10 this ed.
8. Cf. p. 46 of the original; p. 44 this ed.
9. Cf. p. 46 of the original; p. 42 this ed.
10. Cf. p. 47 of the original; p. 43 this ed.
11. Cf. p. 44 of the original; p. 40 this ed.
12. Cf. p. 46 of the original; p. 43 this ed.
13. *Loc. cit.*
14. Cf. p. 48 of the original; p. 44 this ed.
15. Cf. p. 71 of the original; p. 63 this ed.
16. Cf. p. 95 of the original; p. 84 this ed.
17. Cf. p. 108 of the original; p. 97 this ed.
18. Cf. p. 83 of the original; p. 73 this ed.
19. Cf. note 3.
20. I cannot hope in a few short words to make the goal and method of phenomenology completely clear to anyone who is not familiar with it, but must refer all questions arising to Husserl's basic work, the *Ideen*.
21. The use of the term "primordiality" for the act side of experience may attract attention. I employ it because I believe that it has the same character as one attributes to its correlate. I intentionally suppress my usual expression, "actual experience," because I need it for another

phenomenon and wish to avoid equivocation. (This other phenomenon is "act" in the specific sense of experience in the form of "cogito," of "being-turned-toward.")

22. Of course, going over past experiences usually is an "abrégé" of the original course of experience. (In a few minutes I can recapitulate the events of years.) This phenomenon itself merits an investigation of its own.

23. On the concept of neutralization, cf. Husserl's *Ideen*, p. 222ff. [Section 109]

24. It has been stressed repeatedly that the "objectification" of the empathized experience, in contrast with my own experience, is a part of the interpretation of foreign experience, for example, by Desoir (*Beiträge*, p. 477). On the other hand, when [F. A.] Lange (*Wesen der Kunst*, p. 139 ff.) distinguishes between the "subjective illusion of motion," or the motion we intend to perform when faced with an object, and the "object," or the motion we ascribe to the object (perhaps a presented horseman), these are not two independent viewpoints on which completely opposing theories could be built (an aesthetic of empathy and one of illusion) but are the two phases or forms in which empathy can be accomplished as we have described them.

25. [B.] Groethuysen has designated such feeling related to the feelings of others as "fellow feeling" (*Das Mitgefühl*, p. 233). Our use of "fellow feeling," not directed toward foreign feelings but toward their correlate, must be strictly distinguished from his usage. In fellow feeling I am not joyful over the joy of the other but over that over which he is joyful.

26. *Über Annahmen*, p. 233ff.

27. Scheler interprets the understanding of in- (or, as he says, after-) feeling (empathy) and fellow feeling in the same way. *Sympathiegefühle*, p. 4f. [English translation, *The Nature of Sympathy*, London: Peter Heath, 1954]

28. Scheler clearly emphasizes the phenomenon that different people can have strictly the same feeling (*Sympathiegefühle*, pp. 9 and 31) and stresses that the various subjects are thereby retained. However, he does not consider that the unified act does not have the plurality of the individuals for its subject, but a higher unity based on them.

29. *Das Wesen und die Bedeutung der Einfühlung*, p. 33ff.

30. *Zur psychologischen Analyse der ästhetischen Anschauung.*

31. Genetic-psychological investigation here does not mean an investigation of the developmental stages of the psychic individual. Rather, the

stages of psychic development (the types of child, youth, etc.) are included in descriptive psychology. To us genetic psychology and psychology which explains causally are synonymous. On the orientation of psychology to the concept of cause in exact natural science, cf. p. 51 in the following. We distinguish between the two questions: (1) What psychological mechanism functions in the experience of empathy? (2) How has the individual acquired this mechanism in the course of his development? In the genetic theories under discussion this distinction is not always strictly made.

32. Scheler criticizes the theory of imitation (*Sympathiegefühle*, p. 6ff.) He takes exception to it as follows: (1) Imitation presupposes a comprehending expression as expression, exactly what it is to explain. (2) We also understand expressions that we cannot imitate, for example, the expressive movements of animals. (3) We comprehend the inadequacy of an expression, an impossibility if the comprehension occurred by an imitation of the expression alone. (4) We also understand experiences unfamiliar to us from our own earlier experience (for example, mortal terror). This would be impossible if understanding were the reproduction of our own earlier experiences aroused by imitation. These are all objections difficult to refute.

33. For a detailed analysis of the contagion of feeling, see Scheler (*Sympathiegefühle*, p. 11ff.). The only divergence from our view is the contention that the contagion of feeling presupposes no knowledge of the foreign experience at all.

34. A discussion of "mass suggestion" could investigate which of these two (*empathy or sympathy*) is present and to what extent.

35. Scheler raises the point that, in contrast with after-feeling (our empathy), sympathy can be based on remaining in my own reproduced experiences that prevents genuine sympathy from prevailing. (*Sympathiegefühle*, p. 24f.)

36. Biese exaggerates in the opposite direction by asserting, "All associations rest on our ability and compulsion to relate everything to us human beings . . . , to suit the object to ourselves in body and soul." (*Das Assoziationsprinzip und der Anthropomorphismus in der Ästhetik.*)

37. On the intelligibility of expressions, see Part III of this work, Section 7, letter 1, p. 75.

38. Cf. Part III, p. 58.

39. "Symbolbegriff . . . ," p. 76ff.

40. *Die ästhetische Illusion und ihre psychologische Begründung*, p. 10ff.

41. For example, one of the objections raised against this theory is that

it says nothing of wherein this analogy of our own to the foreign body shall consist, the basis of the inference. Only in [G. T.] Fechner do I find a serious attempt to ascertain this. *Zur Seelenfrage*, p. 49f. and p. 63.

42. On the sense in which analogies are justified, see Part III, p. 59.

43. See especially the appendix to *Sympathiegefühle*.

44. Cf. *Sympathiegefühle*, p. 124ff. *Idole*, p. 31.

45. *Idole*, p. 52.

46. *Idole*, p. 42ff.

47. Cf. *Idole*, p. 153.

48. *Resentiment*, p. 42f.

49. *Idole*, p. 63, 118ff.

50. *Idole*, p. 114f.

51. *Idole*, p. 45ff., *Philos. d. Lebens*, p. 173 and 215. A discussion here of his concept of act, which apparently does not coincide with Husserl's, would take us too far.

52. *Idole*, p. 71f. (note).

53. On the nature of reflection, see particularly *Ideen*, p. 72ff. [Section 38]   .

54. *Idole*, p. 112f.

55. I also think that Scheler is inexact when he sometimes calls the false estimation of my experience and of myself that can be based on this deception, a deception of perception.

56. There are differences here, of course. The non-actually perceived feeling, in contrast with the feeling not perceived, certainly is perceived and is an object. On the contrary, feeling has the privilege of remaining conscious in a certain manner even when it is not perceived or comprehended, so that one "is aware of" his feelings. Geiger has precisely analyzed this special manner in which feelings exist in *Bewusstsein von Gefühlen*, p. 152ff.

57. *Idole*, p. 137ff.

58. *Idole*, p. 144ff.

59. *Idole*, p. 130f.

60. *Idole*, p. 75.

61. [H.] Bergson orients himself to this duration of experiences by saying that the past is preserved. All that we experienced endures on into the present, even if only a part of it is currently conscious. (*Evolution créatrice*, p. 5) [*Creative Evolution*, New York: Henry Holt and Company, 1911]

62. These levels of simple noticing, qualitative noticing, and analyzing observation only apply to inner perception and not to reflection, as Geiger says in the work cited.

63. Scheler himself stresses the representational character of comprehended foreign experiences (*Sympathiegefühle*, p. 5), but does not concern
himself with it further and does not return to it at the crucial point (in the
appendix).

64. It is easy to see that this is precluded in principle.

65. Compare [K.] Österreich, *Phänomenologie des Ich*, p. 122f. with
Husserl, *Logische Untersuchungen II*, p. 359ff.

66. I believe that this explains the experience of the "person going two
ways." For example, in his well-known poem, Heine strolls to his be-
loved's house and sees himself standing before the door. This is the
double way of having oneself given in memory or fantasy. Later we shall
consider to what extent a "self"-having is actually present in either case.
Cf. Part II of this work, p. 10 and p. 63 following.

67. Naturally, we should find out what kind of "I" this could be and
whether a world, and what kind of one, could be given to it.

68. Whether a consciousness only exhibiting sensory data and no acts
of the "I" could be regarded "I"-less could certainly still be pondered. In
this case, we could also speak of an "animated" but "I"-less living body.
But I do not believe such an interpretation possible.

69. The expositions in the following part will clarify this point.

70. For more on causality, cf. below, p. 71.

71. In order to prevent misunderstanding, I want to emphasize that I
take "expression" in the above sense and verbal expression for something fundamentally different. At this point I cannot go into the difference but want to call attention to it at the outset to avoid equivocation.

72. We do not need to consider here whether expressive movements
are presented as originally purposeful actions, as Darwin thinks, or as
unconscious and purposeless, as Klages supposes. (*Die Ausdrucksbewegung
und ihre diagnostische Verwertung*, p. 293) At all events, Klages also stresses
the high correlation between the appearance of expression and action.
He says all naive doing and achieving proceeds from experience as easily
and as involuntarily as expressive movements. He considers this instinc-
tive form of action to be the original one, first gradually suppressed by
volition. (p. 366)

In his famous treatise "Über den Ausdruck der Gemütsbewegungen"
Darwin describes bodily appearances that correspond to certain affects,
basing his description on acute observation. Then he seeks to expound
the psycho-physical mechanism by which these bodily processes occur.
He neither considers the descriptive difference between expression and
the appearance of accompaniment, nor does he seriously ask how these
processes are the expressions of the affect they evoke.

73. *Op. cit.*, p. 57f.

74. J. Cohn uses the term "expression" in yet another and still broader sense (*Ästhetik*, p. 56), namely, for everything "outer" in which we perceive an inner life. But here we do not have what we specifically hold to be expression: its motivation.

75. Cf. Husserl's *Ideen*, p. 66. [Section 35]

76. It may seem conspicuous that we have completely omitted the concept usually foremost in other definitions of the individual or organism: the concept of purpose. This has not only been done to keep the presentation from being further burdened by a discussion of the concept of purpose, but also for material reasons. I do not believe that it is possible to speak of an immediately experienced subordination of the psycho-physical occurrence to a unified purpose. This means that the concept of purpose does not come into consideration, either, in the empathic comprehension of a foreign individual.

77. Cf. above p. 42ff.

78. Cf. Part II of this work, p. 6.

79. The phenomenon of fusion may make a genetic explanation of empathy possible. We must only return to our own experience and not speak immediately of the fusion of foreign outer experience with our own.

80. *System der Ästhetik I*, p. 241ff.

81. As already mentioned earlier, [G. T.] Fechner (*Zur Seelenfrage*, p. 49f., 63) has endeavored to lay down the general type forming the basis for all assumptions of animation. (It is not proper to speak of empathy in him.) We cannot go into an examination of his particular statements here. Neither do we want to decide here whether he is justified in including the vegetable kingdom in this type.

82. The word "image" [*Bild*] is a poor metaphor for the interpretation of the spatial world, for an image does not present the world to us, but we see it itself from one side.

83. Cf. the analysis in Husserl's *Ideen*, p. 48f., 60 ff. [Sections 27 and 33]

84. Cf. above p. 41ff.

85. Cf. Part II, p. 18f.

86. Cf. above, p. 10.

87. Cf. *Ideen*, p. 279 and 317. [Section 151]

88. Cf. *Self Consciousness, Social Consciousness and Nature*.

89. Cf. Part II, p. 35f.

90. Since every living body is at the same time a physical body and every alive movement is at the same time mechanical, it is possible to

consider physical bodies and their movements "as if" they were living bodies. This empathizing of movement in the physical body plays a big role in the literature on aesthetic empathy.

91. Even if plants do not possess the voluntary movements of animals, they still essentially possess the phenomenon of growth so that they are comprised of not merely mechanical movement. In addition, they evidence heliotropism and other alive movements.

92. *Sympathiegefühle*, p. 121.

93. Certain phenomena come close to acknowledging sensitivity to light and possibly a certain sensitivity to touch in plants, but I would like to reserve judgment on this.

94. This would make phenomena of life conceivable as non-psychic and plants conceivable as soulless living organisms.

95. *Philosophie des Lebens*, p. 172ff.

96. Cf. *Philosophie des Lebens*.

97. "Causality" here designates the relationship of dependence intuitively comprehended and not the relationship determinable exactly physically.

98. On the question of causality, cf. above, p. 21.

99. Cf. *Idole*, p. 124f.; *Philosophie des Lebens*, p. 218ff.; *Rentenhysterie*, p. 236f. Cf. in the foregoing, Part II, p. 33.

100. We shall here ignore the question of whether "effectiveness" arises in the form of causality or of motivation.

101. *Psychologie*, p. 224. [*The Principles of Psychology*, New York, Henry Holt & Co., 1890.]

102. Even if "co-perceiving" does not fully characterize the phenomenon of expression, it is still important for expression. The experiences we comprehend in expressive appearances are fused with the phenomena of expression. Volkelt has stressed this particularly. (*System der Ästhetik I*, p. 254f., 307). The body's limbs and psychic countenances themselves seem to be animated; the psychic seems to be visible. For example, cheerfulness is visible in laughter, joy in the radiant eyes. The unity of experience and expression is such an inner one that language frequently designates the one by the other: being overcome, weighed down, uplifted. (Cf. Klages, *Die Ausdrucksbewegung und ihre diagnostische Verwertung*, p. 284f.).

103. *Op. cit.*, p. 13.

104. As will be shown later, the terms "sign" [*Zeichen*] and "expression" [*Ausdruck*] are not suitable here. Therefore, we shall speak of "indication" [*Anzeichen*] and "symbol" [*Symbol*]. The following elucidations of the concepts of "indication," "sign," and "expression" are

closely related to Husserl's expositions in his Seminar Exercises of the Winter Semester of 1913-14.

105. [T.] Lipps is probably thinking of this when he concedes that "perception" [*Erfahrung*] is a supplement to empathy.

106. Cf. *Ästhetik II*, p. 2; *Psychologische Untersuchungen II*, p. 448.

107. A change in tone when the meaning is constant, a change of meaning when there is a constant articulation.

108. We can leave out of consideration here cases in which signals function as words or words are used as signals.

109. Klages stresses (*op. cit.*, p. 342) the "expressive" character of language and its original prevalence as such in contrast with its communicative function.

110. For the sake of simplicity, written and printed words will be neglected.

111. In contrast with Lipps, Dohrn's discussion, while going along with him on artistic presentation, has the difference of clearly emphasizing language as the expression of a meaning content and as the externalization or testimony to an experiential content (*op. cit.*, p. 55ff). In this connection, he has characterized poetic types as differing forms of externalization.

112. *Ideen*, p. 89. [Section 47]

113. Roettecken (*Poetik*, p. 22) also calls attention to this kind of empathic deception (and even as the case of deception in the realm of otherwise reliable experience).

114. Thus it is not so incorrect at all when James says that man has as many "social selves" as there are individuals who know him (*Psychologie*, p. 178); only we do not want to accept the designation "social self."

115. On the relationship between fact and essence, factual and essential science, cf. Husserl's *Ideen*, chap. I.

116. If this is protested here, naturally we always intend psychology as the natural scientific psychology prevailing today.

117. This is an interpretation very energetically advocated by Scheler.

118. *Ideen über eine beschreibende und zergliedernde Psychologie.*

119. *Einleitung in die Geisteswissenschaften*, p. 117.

120. *Op. cit.*, p. 136f.

121. *Op. cit.*, p. 47.

122. In his earlier mentioned *Sammelreferat* (p. 48), Geiger has already stressed that reliving understanding as the mere having present of something psychic must be distinguished from empathy. Naturally, he could not undertake a more detailed analysis at that point.

123. Similar distinctions have been made in modern psychopathology

itself. Cf. [K.] Jaspers, "Über kausale and verständliche Zusammenhänge . . ."

124. For evidence of this view in the writing of well-known psychologists, see [T.] Österreich, *Phänomenologie des Ich*, p. 8ff., cf. [P.] Natorp, too, *Allgemeine Psychologie*, p. 52.

125. Moreover, the same turning is also needed to "objectify" the correlate of an act of feeling. (Cf. Husserl's *Ideen*, p. 66). [Section 35] For example, it is accomplished by the transition from valuing, the primordial feeling of a value, to the value judgment.

126. I cannot entirely agree with [M.] Geiger when he denies sensory feelings all "participation in the 'I'" (*Phänomenologie des äesthetischen Genusses*, p. 613f.). If, as one must, one distinguishes the pleasantness of sensation from the pleasure it gives me, then I do not see how one can strike the "I"-moment from this pleasure. Of course, neither can I see Geiger's distinction between pleasure and enjoyment insofar as it is based on participation in the "I." Further, I cannot acknowledge that there is no negative counterpart to enjoyment (such as displeasure to pleasure, dislike to liking). It seems to me that a more detailed analysis should be able to expose suffering as the negative counterpart of enjoyment.

127. On the hierarchy of values, cf. Scheler *Der Formalismus in der Ethik usw.*, p. 488ff.

128. On the relationship between height and duration of values, cf. Scheler, *op. cit.*, p. 492ff.

129. *Motiv und Motivation*, p. 169.

130. [A.] Pfänder, *op. cit.*, p. 168.

131. Pfänder, *op. cit.*, p. 174.

132. *Beiträge zum Studium der Individualität*, p. 327ff.

133. Meyer also notes the "necessity" of re-experiencing (*Stilgesetz der Poetik*, p. 29ff.), but without keeping the lawfulness of meaning and causal lawfulness separated.

134. E. v. Hartmann in his *Ästhetik* has characterized the relationship between the psycho-physical and the spiritual individual somewhat as we have tried to do it here. (II, p. 190ff., 200ff.). For him every individual is an empirical realization of an "individual idea."

135. *Beiträge sum Studium der Individualität*, p. 300.

136. There is a corresponding ontic lawfulness to which the correlate of these acts, the relationships of value and ought, are subject. (What is valuable ought to be.) But we need not go into this here.

137. See above, p. 103f.

138. The fact that every individual and every one of his concrete

experiences is plainly an experience happening only once does not contradict the typicalness of personal structure because the content of a number of streams of consciousness cannot in principle be the same.

139. Of course, Dilthey also conceives of the concept of type as at first not spiritual, but as psychic. This becomes very obvious in his description of the poetic type which, for the most part, consists of a definite peculiarity of psycho-physical organization: sharpness and liveliness of perception and memories, intensity of experience, etc. (*Die Einbildungskraft des Dichters*, p. 344ff.). On the contrary, other traits he presents indicate the peculiarity of a typical personal structure. This is seen in the expression of experience in the creative performance of fantasy. (*Über die Einbildungskraft der Dichter*, p. 66f.)

Index

131

The Institute of Carmelite Studies promotes research and publication in the field of Carmelite spirituality. Its members are Discalced Carmelites, part of a Roman Catholic community—friars, nuns and laity—who are heirs to the teaching and way of life of Teresa of Jesus and John of the Cross, men and women dedicated to contemplation and to ministry in the Church and the world. Information concerning their way of life is available through local diocesan Vocation Offices, or from the Vocation Director's Office, 1525 Carmel Road, Hubertus, WI 53033.